HANDEL'S "MESSIAH"

STEPHEN J. BINZ

TWENTY-THIRD PUBLICATIONS
977 Hartford Turnpike Unit A
Waterford, CT 06385
(860) 437-3012 or (800) 321-0411
twentythirdpublications.com

Copyright ©2025 Stephen J. Binz. All rights reserved. No part of this publication may be reproduced in any manner without prior written permission of the publisher. Write to the Permissions Editor.

The Scripture passages contained herein are from the *New Revised Standard Version Bible,* Catholic edition. Copyright ©1989, by the Division of Christian Education of the National Council of the Churches of Christ in the U.S.A. All rights reserved.

Image credit: page xii - stock.adobe.com

ISBN: 978-1-62785-844-1
Printed in the U.S.A.

What People Are Saying about *Threshold Bible Study*

"In *Threshold Bible Study*, Stephen Binz provides the tools and an effective process for deep reflection on specific themes developed in different ways across the fullness of scriptural texts. His approach is rich, multidimensional, and very challenging—a gift to all of us who yearn to be disciples of Christ!"

■ **Marie Dennis**, *Former President of Pax Christi International, Chair of Catholic Nonviolence Initiative*

"Small groups where men and women of faith can gather to reflect and support each other are essential for the New Evangelization. Stephen Binz has a proven record of supplying excellent resource material to help these groups break open the Scriptures and be nourished and renewed by the living word of God. I commend him for continuing to provide this important service with the *Threshold Bible Study* series."

■ **Archbishop Paul-André Durocher**, *Archbishop of Gatineau, Quebec*

"*Threshold Bible Study* is an attractive and accessible way to help Catholics read and cherish Scripture in the context of our tradition. The word of God has the power to transform believers into more active disciples of Jesus Christ and to enrich their faith through the working of the Holy Spirit. For this reason, I encourage Bible study in every parish because if we don't offer it, we can be sure that people will look elsewhere to find ways of studying and savoring God's nourishing word."

■ **Archbishop Shelton J. Fabre**, *Archbishop of Louisville*

"In the volumes of his *Threshold Bible Study*, Stephen Binz gives us a rich treasury for nurturing our faith with the power of the biblical word. Besides his fine Bible scholarship, what I like most is the engaging pedagogy that he provides toward group conversation and faith sharing, welcoming the contribution of each participant. While honoring the legacy of the time-tested *lectio divina*, Binz recrafts this soul-engaging process for busy people in our time, encouraging all to reflect and share our faith—the most likely way to grow it."

■ **Dr. Thomas Groome**, *Professor of Theology and Religious Education, Boston College*

"*Threshold Bible Study* is a terrific resource for parishes, groups, and individuals who desire to delve more deeply into Scripture and Church teaching. Stephen J. Binz has created guides which are profound yet also accessible and which answer the growing desire among today's laity for tools to grow in both faith and community."

■ **Lisa M. Hendey**, *Author and Founder of CatholicMom.com*

"Stephen Binz provides the Church with a tremendous gift and resource in the *Threshold Bible Study*. This great series invites readers into the world of Scripture with insight, wisdom, and accessibility. This series will help you fall in love with the word of God!"
■ **Dr. Daniel P. Horan**, *Director of the Center for Spirituality and Professor at Saint Mary's College, South Bend*

"Inviting, accessible, and wise, *Threshold Bible Study* is an absolutely superb resource for all Catholics interested in unlocking the living word. You now have no excuse not to read and enjoy the Bible."
■ **James Martin, SJ**, *Editor-at-large at America Media, Author of* ***Jesus: A Pilgrimage***

"*Threshold Bible Study* is an enriching and enlightening approach to understanding the rich faith which the Scriptures hold for us today. Written in a clear and concise style, *Threshold Bible Study* presents solid contemporary biblical scholarship, offers questions for reflection and/or discussion, and then demonstrates a way to pray from the Scriptures. All these elements work together to offer the reader a wonderful insight into how the sacred texts of our faith can touch our lives in a profound and practical way today. I heartily recommend this series to both individuals and Bible study groups."
■ **Gregory J. Polan, OSB**, *Conception Abbey, Abbot Primate of the Benedictine Order*

"Stephen J. Binz is a consistently outstanding Catholic educator and communicator whose books on the study and application of Scripture have thoroughly enriched my Christian understanding. In our fast-moving, often-confusing times, his ability to help us examine and comprehend the truth through all the noise is especially needed and valuable."
■ **Elizabeth Scalia**, *Writer and Speaker, Blogger as The Anchoress*

"Stephen Binz has created an essential resource for the New Evangelization rooted in the discipleship process that helps participants to unpack the treasures of the Scriptures in an engaging and accessible manner. *Threshold Bible Study* connects faith learning to faithful living, leading one to a deeper relationship with Christ and his body, the Church."
■ **Julianne Stanz**, *Director of Outreach for Evangelization and Discipleship for Loyola Press*

"*Threshold Bible Study* draws readers into an experience of the word of God through intricately researched historical details along with a profound spirituality of the Scriptures. Encountering Christ through the word provides light for our lives, hope for our hearts, and passion to share this word with everyone. Thanks to Stephen Binz's scholarship, readers can delve deeply into God's love letter to humanity!"
■ **Sr. Nancy Usselmann, FSP**, *Director of Pauline Center for Media Studies*

Contents

LESSONS 13–18

LESSONS 19–24

LESSONS 25–30

How to Use *Threshold Bible Study*

Each book in the *Threshold Bible Study* series is designed to lead you through a new doorway of biblical awareness, to accompany you across a unique threshold of understanding. The characters, places, and images that you encounter in each of these topical studies will help you explore fresh dimensions of your faith and discover richer insights for your spiritual life.

Threshold Bible Study covers biblical themes in depth in a short amount of time. Unlike more traditional Bible studies that treat a biblical book or series of books, *Threshold Bible Study* aims to address specific topics within the entire Bible. The goal is not for you to comprehend everything about each passage, but rather for you to understand what a variety of passages from different books of the Bible reveals about the topic of each study.

Threshold Bible Study offers you an opportunity to explore the entire Bible from the viewpoint of a variety of different themes. The commentary that follows each biblical passage launches your reflection about that passage and helps you begin to see its significance within the context of your contemporary experience. The questions following the commentary challenge you to understand the passage more fully and apply it to your own life. The prayer starter helps conclude your study by integrating learning into your relationship with God.

These studies are designed for maximum flexibility. Each study is presented in a workbook format, with sections for reading, reflecting, writing, discussing, and praying. Space for writing after each question is ideal for personal study and allows group members to prepare in advance for their discussion. The thirty lessons in each topic may be used by an individual over the period of a month, or by a group for six sessions, with lessons to be studied each week before the next group meeting. These studies are ideal for Bible study groups, small Christian communities, adult faith formation, student groups, Sunday school, neighborhood groups, and family reading, as well as for individual learning.

The method of *Threshold Bible Study* is rooted in the classical tradition of *lectio divina*, an ancient yet contemporary means for reading the Scriptures reflectively and prayerfully. Reading and interpreting the text (*lectio*) is followed by reflective meditation on its message (*meditatio*). This reading and reflecting flows into prayer from the heart (*oratio* and *contemplatio*).

This ancient method assures us that Bible study is a matter of both the mind and the heart. It is not just an intellectual exercise to learn more and be able to discuss the Bible with others. It is, more important, a transforming experience. Reflecting on God's word, guided by the Holy Spirit, illumines the mind with wisdom and stirs the heart with zeal.

Following the personal Bible study, *Threshold Bible Study* offers a method for extending *lectio divina* into a weekly conversation with a small group. This communal experience will allow participants to enhance their appreciation of the message and build up a spiritual community (*collatio*). The end result will be to increase not only individual faith but also faithful witness in the context of daily life (*operatio*).

Through the spiritual disciplines of Scripture reading, study, reflection, conversation, and prayer, *Threshold Bible Study* will help you experience God's grace more abundantly and root your life more deeply in Christ. The risen Jesus said: "Listen! I am standing at the door, knocking; if you hear my voice and open the door, I will come in to you and eat with you, and you with me" (Rev 3:20). Listen to the word of God, open the door, and cross the threshold to an unimaginable dwelling with God!

SUGGESTIONS FOR INDIVIDUAL STUDY

- Make your Bible reading a time of prayer. Ask for God's guidance as you read the Scriptures.
- Try to study daily, or as often as possible according to the circumstances of your life.
- Read the Bible passage carefully, trying to understand both its meaning and its personal application as you read. Some persons find it helpful to read the passage aloud.
- Read the passage in another Bible translation. Each version adds to your understanding of the original text.
- Allow the commentary to help you comprehend and apply the scriptural text. The commentary is only a beginning, not the last word, on the meaning of the passage.
- After reflecting on each question, write out your responses. The very act of writing will help you clarify your thoughts, bring new insights, and amplify your understanding.
- As you reflect on your answers, think about how you can live God's word in the context of your daily life.
- Conclude each daily lesson by reading the prayer and continuing with your own prayer from the heart.
- Make sure your reflections and prayers are matters of both the mind and the heart. A true encounter with God's word is always a transforming experience.
- Choose a word or a phrase from the lesson to carry with you throughout the day as a reminder of your encounter with God's life-changing word.
- For additional insights and affirmation, share your learning experience with at least one other person whom you trust. The ideal way to share learning is in a small group that meets regularly.

SUGGESTIONS FOR GROUP STUDY

- Meet regularly; weekly is ideal. Try to be on time and make attendance a high priority for the sake of the group. The average group meets for about an hour.
- Open each session with a prepared prayer, a song, or a reflection. Find some appropriate way to bring the group from the workaday world into a sacred time of graced sharing.
- If you have not been together before, name tags are very helpful as a group begins to become acquainted with the other group members.
- Spend the first session getting acquainted with one another, reading the Introduction aloud, and discussing the questions that follow.
- Appoint a group facilitator to provide guidance to the discussion. The role of facilitator may rotate among members each week. The facilitator simply keeps the discussion on track; each person shares responsibility for the group. There is no need for the facilitator to be a trained teacher.
- Try to study the six lessons on your own during the week. When you have done your own reflection and written your own answers, you will be better prepared to discuss the six scriptural lessons with the group. If you have not had an opportunity to study the passages during the week, meet with the group anyway to share support and insights.
- Participate in the discussion as much as you are able, offering your thoughts, insights, feelings, and decisions. You learn by sharing with others the fruits of your study.
- Be careful not to dominate the discussion. It is important that everyone in the group be offered an equal opportunity to share the results of their work. Try to link what you say to the comments of others so that the group remains on the topic.
- When discussing your own personal thoughts or feelings, use "I" language. Be as personal and honest as appropriate and be very cautious about giving advice to others.

- Listen attentively to the other members of the group so as to learn from their insights. The words of the Bible affect each person in a different way, so a group provides a wealth of understanding for each member.
- Don't fear silence. Silence in a group is as important as silence in personal study. It allows individuals time to listen to the voice of God's Spirit and the opportunity to form their thoughts before they speak.
- Solicit several responses for each question. The thoughts of different people will build on the answers of others and will lead to deeper insights for all.
- Don't fear controversy. Differences of opinions are a sign of a healthy and honest group. If you cannot resolve an issue, continue on, agreeing to disagree. There is probably some truth in each viewpoint.
- Discuss the questions that seem most important for the group. There is no need to cover all the questions in the group session.
- Realize that some questions about the Bible cannot be resolved, even by experts. Don't get stuck on some issue for which there are no clear answers.
- Whatever is said in the group is said in confidence and should be regarded as such.
- Pray as a group in whatever way feels comfortable. Pray for the members of your group throughout the week.

Schedule for Group Study

SESSION 1: INTRODUCTION DATE: ____________

SESSION 2: LESSONS 1–6 DATE: ____________

SESSION 3: LESSONS 7–12 DATE: ____________

SESSION 4: LESSONS 13–18 DATE: ____________

SESSION 5: LESSONS 19–24 DATE: ____________

SESSION 6: LESSONS 25–30 DATE: ____________

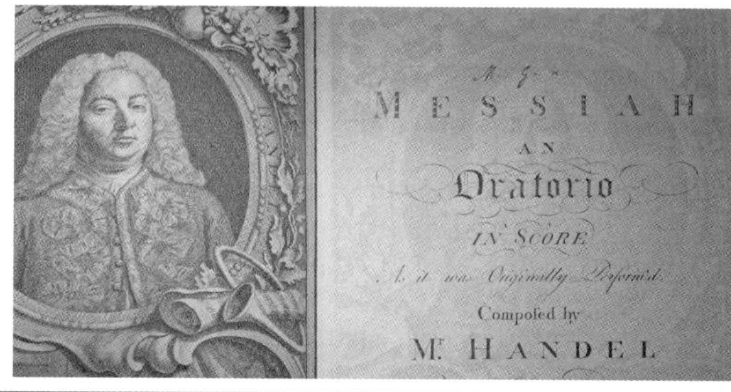
MESSIAH
AN
Oratorio
IN SCORE
As it was Originally Perform'd
Compofed by
Mr. HANDEL

INTRODUCTION  SESSION 1

I know that my Redeemer lives, and that at the last he will stand upon the earth; and after my skin has been thus destroyed, then in my flesh I shall see God, whom I shall see on my side, and my eyes shall behold, and not another. JOB 19:25–27

Handel's *Messiah*

Truth, goodness, and beauty find their source in God and become a guide to the Christian quest: seeking to believe what is true, imitate what is good, and behold what is beautiful. The inspired Scriptures offer these three transcendent virtues, and all who hear the sacred texts must pursue them in order to experience the fullness of God's word. For indeed, the Christian message is both persuasive and attractive, convincing and enticing.

For the masses of Christians through the ages, most of whom were illiterate and therefore unable to read the biblical texts, oral proclamation, vocal music, and visual art have presented the biblical story of salvation. *Messiah*, by George Frideric Handel (1685–1759), is a fairly recent expression in light of the church's long tradition of musical and artistic creations, yet this scriptural masterpiece expresses the Bible's sacred texts in a beautiful way, allowing us to experience the splendor of the word of God. Like all genuine beauty, *Messiah* awakens our spirit and opens us to transcendence.

In creating his biblical music, Handel interpreted the Scriptures in such a way as to produce a melodious masterpiece. His meditation on the word of God and his spiritual vision produced *Messiah*. Likewise, as we meditate on these same texts, we can be inspired and motivated by their profound meaning to produce a beautiful life.

As a musical work grows within the imagination of a Christian artist in response to Scripture, so saints grow within the womb of the church through their response to God's word. And just as a beautiful work of art can evangelize, our lives can announce the good news by the ways we respond to the magnificence we discover in the word of God. As sacred music can be a hearing of the gospel, we too can be God's work of art by reflecting and witnessing to God's saving love.

Handel's *Messiah* proclaims the central truths of the Christian faith: hope for the Messiah, the death and resurrection of Jesus Christ, and the eternal life which he brings to the world. Because the words of *Messiah* are also God's living word, they captivate us and move us to receive God's grace. Handel's work is exceptionally beautiful because it expresses and proclaims Jesus Christ, who is divine beauty incarnate, and draws us into his kingdom.

Reflection and discussion

- Why is music such an important part of religious experience?

- When has a work of music moved my heart in some profound way?

A Musical Panorama of Redemption

Messiah is one of the most performed and listened to musical compositions of the past three centuries. Nearly everyone is able to recognize at least some of the melodies of this familiar and beloved work of sacred music. All of its texts are from the Scriptures, and they are designed to do nothing less than tell the story of the world's redemption through Jesus the Messiah.

Handel's work opens before us a vast panorama, beginning with the hope-filled voice of the prophet promising salvation and ending at the doorway of heaven as a chorus of angels celebrates Christ's accomplishment. By illuminating the meaning of the biblical texts of Handel's work, this study will enhance both our musical enjoyment and our understanding of God's saving plan. By meditatively listening to both the inspired Scripture and the beautiful music of *Messiah,* we are offered the opportunity to open the door of our hearts and cross the threshold into a more abundant experience of God's transforming love.

Messiah was first performed during the Lent and Easter seasons, though today it is frequently presented in the Advent and Christmas seasons. But it is appropriate for any season of the liturgical year and can be experienced at any time because it tells the whole story, from the dawning of salvation to its glorious completion. Listening to the texts and tunes of *Messiah* offers a profound reflection on the mystery and purposes of God for the entire world. Just as Handel's masterpiece has moved the hearts of millions before us, it can transform us anew through expressing the power of God's grace in the world.

This Bible study includes the 53 movements of *Messiah* and divides the entire libretto into thirty lessons. Each contains the words of the libretto with Handel's original texts taken from his seventeenth-century translation of the Bible. Then Handel's text is followed by a larger passage of Scripture containing the context of Handel's biblical text in a contemporary translation.

To enjoy the music along with this study, obtain one of the many fine recordings of *Messiah* and play it section by section as you study each movement. Make sure you have the unabridged *Messiah,* since many recordings offer only selected portions. Though the music is not necessary for a study of these beautiful Scriptures, it can certainly add to the enjoyment, provide a magnificent entry into a study of the inspired texts, and amplify the spiritual experience of this study.

Since Handel made numerous changes to the score of his oratorio from its first performance until his death, there is no definitive version of *Messiah.* Recordings will vary slightly from one to another, depending on the edition used and the individual interpretations of different performers and conductors. The printed libretto and the numbering of the musical movements will also vary slightly among the various versions of the score. However, the variations will not be significant enough to cause confusion in the daily selection of music and text for listening and study.

This study is ideal for choruses performing *Messiah* or congregations preparing to hear it. It is also a wonderful study for anyone during the seasons of Advent, Christmas, Lent, and Easter. At the end, listeners and readers will have a sense that they have personally experienced the drama of redemption.

Through stirring music and inspired texts, they will experience God's saving plan to rescue a lost and exiled humanity. They will feel the bright dawn lighting up the darkness, the hope of liberation entering their imprisoned spirit, and the confidence that God's love instills.

Reflection and discussion

- Which of *Messiah*'s tunes are most familiar to me?

- Why is Handel's *Messiah* appropriate for any time of the year?

Composing and Performing *Messiah*

George Frideric Handel was born in Halle in northern Germany but made his career in London. He composed and produced Italian operas for many years, then began to create oratorios as the musical tastes of the English changed. Eventually, Handel wrote a whole series of oratorios based on biblical themes and texts. Among them are *Samson, Israel in Egypt, Saul,* and, of course, *Messiah.*

An oratorio is like an opera in that it is a sung musical drama. But unlike opera, the oratorio does not have costumes, acting, and lavish scenery. Its production consists of a chorus, orchestra, and soloists. The chorus stands behind the orchestra, and the soloists stand closest to the audience. Handel's earliest oratorios were written to be performed during Lent, when the theaters were ordinarily closed and opera was forbidden because of the season's solemnity. Handel convinced the bishop of London to allow the performance of his oratorios because of their biblical subjects and their lack of costuming and elaborate detail. Most of the criticism of *Messiah* at the time had nothing to do with the music; it involved Handel's use of a sacred subject for musical entertainment in a theater.

Like opera, oratorios are composed of a series of movements called recitatives, arias, and choruses. A recitative is a rhythmically free vocal style that imitates the natural inflections of speech. It is sung by a soloist with simple chordal accompaniment and is used to advance the narrative. An aria is an elaborate melody sung by a soloist accompanied by the orchestra. A chorus is sung by many voices, often providing the oratorio's most climactic and powerful moments.

The libretto, the biblical text for *Messiah,* was written by Charles Jennens, an English aristocrat with an interest in theology. The texts were taken primarily from the King James Bible, though a few of the psalms reflect an earlier translation used in the Anglican Book of Common Prayer. Many of the texts were drawn from the lectionary for Advent, Lent, and Eastertide, but Jennens' selection and arrangement of the texts are unique and masterful. Though extracted from many different sections of the Bible, each text segues beautifully into the next. The biblical selections also reflect a sensitive understanding of the musical demands of the work as they alternate nicely among recitatives, arias, and choruses.

Handel wrote *Messiah* at a feverish pace between August 22 and September 14, 1741. Depriving himself of much food and sleep, Handel's zealous fervor is explained by the combination of ecstatic inspiration and the need for money. His speed is also due to the fact that Handel recycled much of his own music from previous works as well as melodies from other composers, a common practice at the time. Part of Handel's genius lay in his ability to transform other works for totally new purposes. At the end of his 259-page score, Handel inscribed the letters SDG, abbreviating *Solo Deo Gloria,* "To God alone the glory."

After completing *Messiah,* Handel accepted an invitation to give a series of charity performances in Dublin. He left for Dublin in November with his musicians, and after a series of a dozen concerts, he unveiled *Messiah* on April 13, 1742. The first performance of *Messiah* was an eagerly attended social event. Seven hundred people crowded into the music hall on Fishamble Street. To make sure everyone could fit into the auditorium, the advertisement for the event requested that the ladies not wear hoop skirts and that gentlemen leave their fashionable swords at home. Hundreds were turned away that evening, so *Messiah* was performed in Dublin again in June before Handel returned home.

The first performance in London was given the next spring. Beginning in 1750, Handel conducted annual performances to benefit the Foundling

Hospital, and soon his oratorio held a firm place in the hearts of the English people. *Messiah* was Handel's last public performance in 1759, eight days before his death. His tomb in Westminster Abbey is inscribed with the words of one of *Messiah*'s most beautiful arias, "I know that my Redeemer liveth."

Reflection and discussion

- In what way is the musical form of oratorio somewhere between opera and church music?

- In what way do I experience singing as a form of prayer? How does singing with others in a choir, chorus, or church service create an experience of joyful worship?

Messiah's Biblical Texts

The libretto of *Messiah* consists entirely of biblical texts, arranged in such a way that the listener experiences the drama of redemption from start to finish. Its seventy-three biblical verses include forty-three from the Old Testament and thirty from the New Testament. Yet, though the work is truly about Jesus Christ, it is not a narrative text describing his teachings, miracles, or the formation of his disciples. In fact, only ten of its many biblical verses are taken from the gospels. *Messiah*, rather, is a reflective commentary on the meaning of Christ's life for us. It shines a spotlight on the saving significance of his coming into the world and of his redemptive passion, death, and resurrection.

The biblical passages chosen for *Messiah* might be compared to the stained glass windows of a gothic church. As each window encapsulates a very complex history and theology into a single luminous panel, so each musical text makes an entire scriptural theme radiantly present before us. A gothic church surrounds us with sacred history, making it shine upon us; *Messiah* tells the story of salvation concisely, just a couple of verses at a time, in a way that allows us to take in its essence and to experience its significance for ourselves.

The biblical passages chosen for *Messiah* illustrate how inspired texts convey a variety of meanings. Since most of the verses in *Messiah* are from the Old Testament, clearly these texts did not originally refer to the life of Jesus, but rather to historical circumstances within the life of ancient Israel. Yet, within the context of the whole Christian Bible, these ancient texts take on new and fuller meaning. Christian believers understand the meaning of these ancient texts to be fulfilled in the coming of Israel's Messiah.

St. Augustine explained, "The New Testament lies hidden in the Old, and the Old Testament is unveiled in the New." *Messiah*'s application of Old Testament texts to Christ is a perfect example of Augustine's statement. The oratorio is not so much taking these passages out of context as it is expressing the new context in which these ancient verses take on new meaning. This is exactly what the early Christians and the long history of Christian theology have done. Ancient texts are understood in new ways. Because the Holy Spirit has inspired the entire Bible, all Scripture has fuller meaning in light of the saving life of Jesus the Messiah.

Since biblical passages have multiple layers of meaning, as old texts are interpreted in new contexts, biblical readers must try to understand the fullness of meaning in a text. Sometimes, in an attempt to be true to the original context of Israel's literature, we neglect to emphasize the new Christian meaning of a passage. But at other times, we become so accustomed to the Christian meaning of a passage that we forget about its original meaning in ancient Israel. For example, when we hear the words of Isaiah "For unto us a child is born, unto us a son is given" (Isa 9:6), we tend to think immediately of the birth of Jesus in Bethlehem. But this prophecy of Isaiah has a long history that predates the coming of Jesus by many centuries. When we fail to explore its long history and its multiple layers of meaning, we miss the depth and richness of the biblical passage.

Handel's *Messiah* explores both the original and the fuller meanings of many biblical texts of Advent, Lent, and the Easter season. Understanding the meanings intended by their original human authors offers us a new depth of awareness through which we can better comprehend what these words tell us about Jesus Christ. And then, having understood how these passages have been comprehended by believers through the ages in light of their own situations, we are better able to appreciate how they apply to our own lives today. The result will be a fuller understanding of Scripture as the living word of our God.

Handel divided his oratorio into three parts. Part 1 is concerned with God's promise of the Messiah to fill the deep longings of the human race. The promise is answered in the birth of Jesus and his saving ministry. Part 2 proclaims the Messiah's work of redemption through his passion, death, and resurrection. The Messiah's saving accomplishments result in his exaltation and eternal reign. Part 3 applies the Messiah's saving deeds to our own lives with the promise of resurrection and everlasting life.

Reflection and discussion

- In what ways are the biblical texts of *Messiah* like the stained glass windows of biblical scenes in a church? Why is meditation the most appropriate response to these texts?

- How do we limit the richness of biblical verses by looking at their meaning in only one context?

Prayer

God of freedom and life, you have heard the cries of your people and sent the Messiah to rescue your people from darkness and exile. Stir my heart to cry out to you in my struggles and give me hope to turn to you as my Redeemer. As I listen to the words and music of Messiah, *work deeply within me to give me confidence in your saving will for my life and for all the people of the earth. Enlighten and encourage me as I hear and contemplate your inspired word in these sacred Scriptures. Show me how to make my life a testimony to your saving love.*

SUGGESTIONS FOR FACILITATORS, GROUP SESSION 1

1. If the group is meeting for the first time, or if there are newcomers joining the group, it is helpful to provide nametags.

2. Distribute the books to the members of the group.

3. You may want to ask the participants to introduce themselves and tell the group a bit about themselves.

4. Ask one or more of these introductory questions:
   - What drew you to join this group?
   - What is your biggest fear in beginning this Bible study?
   - How is beginning this study like a "threshold" for you?

5. You may want to pray this prayer as a group:
   Come upon us, Holy Spirit, to enlighten and guide us as we begin this study of Handel's Messiah. *You inspired the biblical authors to express your word as manifested to the people of Israel and most fully in the life of Jesus. Motivate us each day to read the Scriptures and deepen our understanding and love for these sacred texts. Bless us during this session and throughout the coming week with the fire of your love.*

6. Read the Introduction aloud, pausing at each question for discussion. Group members may wish to write down the insights of the group as each question is discussed. Encourage several members of the group to respond to each question.

7. Don't feel compelled to finish the complete Introduction during the session. It is better to allow sufficient time to talk about the questions raised than to rush to the end. Group members may read any remaining sections on their own after the group meeting.

8. Instruct group members to read the first six lessons on their own during the six days before the next group meeting. They should write out their own answers to the questions as preparation for next week's group discussion.

9. Fill in the date for each group meeting under "Schedule for Group Study."

10. Conclude by praying aloud together the prayer at the end of the Introduction.

But as for me, I will look to the Lord, I will wait for the God of my salvation; my God will hear me. MICAH 7:7

The Hope of God's People

1. OVERTURE (orchestra)

Listening to Handel's overture, we sense a deep longing within the hearts of our spiritual ancestors to experience what God is going to do next in the world. The Hebrew people held in Egyptian bondage yearned to be liberated from slavery. The people of Judah languishing in exile longed to be released to return to their homeland. The Jewish people experiencing Roman domination in the days of King Herod desired a new kingdom that only a descendant of David could bring. As we listen in the darkness to the somber chords of the overture, we too experience spiritual gloom tinged with a glimmer of hope.

As *Messiah*'s overture crescendos to its climax, hope is amplified. We know that God has not abandoned his people or forsaken his ancient promises. God is going to act again in the history of his people and display his faithfulness. Israel's hope will not go unfulfilled; a new beginning is on the horizon.

"Messiah" comes from a Hebrew word meaning "anointed one." While used occasionally to describe priests and prophets in the Bible, the anointed one refers primarily to Israel's kings. At the installation to the office, a priest would take a ram's horn filled with olive oil and pour it over the head of the one God appointed to lead his people. In later writings of the Jewish people, the Messiah referred to a future king from the lineage of King

David who would liberate God's people from bondage and bring them true freedom and peace.

After the reign of David, the kingship in Israel suffered decline. The kings were not always just or wise; they often failed to bring victory and peace. In fact, the gap between the praise and honor extolled upon Israel's Messiah in the psalms and prophets and the historical reality of Israel's kings increasingly widened. But within this chasm grew the hope that someday a worthy successor to David would come to the throne and God's people would be ruled with justice and know God's peace.

Whenever God's people were oppressed, the words of God's prophets and inspired texts would resonate with new hope for the Messiah. So it was when the disciples of Jesus read the ancient texts. They saw in Jesus the fulfillment of their hopes. In him they found a greater fulfillment of the ancient Scriptures than the prophets ever imagined. The kingdom of this Son of David would have no end, and he would reign forever and ever.

Jesus is the anointed one whom Handel's *Messiah* proclaims. Yet, throughout the performance, we never hear the name of Jesus or hear his teachings. The scriptural texts, rather, speak indirectly about the redeeming mission of the Messiah. The oratorio encourages us to reflect on the meaning of the Messiah's redeeming mission, the liberation of his people, and his everlasting kingdom.

Reflection and discussion

- In what ways do my thoughts and emotions change and develop throughout the length of *Messiah*'s wordless overture?

- What are my deepest longings? How do I experience hope?

- What are the messianic hopes of ancient Israel that Jesus perfectly fulfilled?

- What are my hopes and anticipations as I begin this new study?

Prayer

Saving God, all people long for your deliverance and peace in the depths of their hearts. Stir up hope within me so that I may trust in your ancient promises and place my confidence in your redeeming power.

Every valley shall be lifted up, and every mountain and hill be made low; the uneven ground shall become level, and the rough places a plain. ISAIAH 40:4

Preparing the Way for the Lord

2. RECITATIVE (Tenor)

Comfort ye, comfort ye my people, saith your God; speak ye comfortably to Jerusalem; and cry unto her, that her warfare is accomplished, that her iniquity is pardoned. The voice of him that crieth in the wilderness: Prepare ye the way of the Lord, make straight in the desert a highway for our God. (Isaiah 40:1–3)

3. ARIA (Tenor)

Every valley shall be exalted, and every mountain and hill made low, the crooked straight and the rough places plain. (Isaiah 40:4)

4. CHORUS

And the glory of the Lord shall be revealed, and all flesh shall see it together, for the mouth of the Lord hath spoken it. (Isaiah 40:5)

ISAIAH 40:1–8

1 *Comfort, O comfort my people,*
says your God.
2 *Speak tenderly to Jerusalem,*
and cry to her

that she has served her term,
that her penalty is paid,
that she has received from the Lord's hand
double for all her sins.

3 *A voice cries out:*
"In the wilderness prepare the way of the Lord,
make straight in the desert a highway for our God.
4 *Every valley shall be lifted up,*
and every mountain and hill be made low;
the uneven ground shall become level,
and the rough places a plain.
5 *Then the glory of the Lord shall be revealed,*
and all people shall see it together,
for the mouth of the Lord has spoken."

6 *A voice says, "Cry out!"*
And I said, "What shall I cry?"
All people are grass,
their constancy is like the flower of the field.
7 *The grass withers, the flower fades,*
when the breath of the Lord blows upon it;
surely the people are grass.
8 *The grass withers, the flower fades;*
but the word of our God will stand forever.

The music begins softly but conveys the confident hope that God is beginning to do something new among his people. The tenor expresses God's reassuring message, "Comfort ye my people." The time of warfare is definitively ended and the sins of God's people are forgiven. The music soars, expressing the hope arising in the hearts of God's people and the confidence God's message offers.

These words of the prophet Isaiah were first spoken to the community of Judah who had been taken into exile by their Babylonian conquerors. In the worst disaster of their history, God's people had been deported from their homeland while their beloved city and temple had been destroyed. They had lost nearly everything that gave them identity, and it seemed as though God had abandoned them.

Into this utter desolation, God speaks words of great consolation. God is instructing his emissaries to convey the message of comfort, pardon, and redemption to the broken community. The divine words "Comfort, O comfort my people" (verse 1) have a calming sound and rhythm, especially in the original Hebrew, like a parent soothing a child after a bad dream: "It's all right. It's all over." God assures his people that the period of suffering under which Israel had experienced so much loss and shame has come to an end (verse 2). Through Israel's repentance and God's forgiveness, peace has returned, and God will again answer the promises he had given through the intimate bond of Israel's covenant.

Isaiah presents the image of a highway built straight across the desert from Babylon to Jerusalem (verse 3). Metaphorically, the desert represents our world filled with strife and iniquity, but God will travel that broad road in the wilderness, leading his people home. But if the Lord is to come and rescue his people, there is serious preparatory work to be done. The way must be prepared, obstacles need to be removed, and deceitful bends need to be straightened (verse 4). This processional highway expresses the restoration experienced by God's exiled people as God graciously reenters their history.

This preparation of God's people in the days of Isaiah and their exile serves as a model for the preparatory repentance that was needed once again five centuries later as the coming of the Messiah approached. All four gospels begin the story of Jesus' saving ministry with the witness of John the Baptist and his call to repentance. These words of Isaiah are reinterpreted by the gospel writers and form the very words John the Baptist proclaims as he calls people to prepare their lives for the advent of Jesus Christ (see Luke 3:3–6).

The tenor aria jubilantly describes the construction of the highway for God in the desert. Each phrase of the aria is tonally shaped to musically express its poetic images. The singer bursts forth with agile, ornamented passages as he contrasts the exaltation of the valleys and the lowering of the mountains and hills. These coloratura passages add intensity and drama. The word "valley" ends on a low note, while "exalted" forms a rising melody. "Mountain" forms a peak in the melody, and "hill" a smaller one, while "low" is sung on another low note. "Crooked" is sung rapidly with four disjunct notes, while "straight" is sung on a single tone, and in "the rough places plain," the final word, "plain," is extended through a series of long notes which express the expansive way constructed for God and his people to travel home.

The buoyant chorus expresses the ultimate purpose of God's coming to redeem his people: the glory of God will be revealed to all humanity (verse 5). It is appropriate that this revelation to all people—"all flesh shall see it together"—should be the first verse sung by the chorus. Isaiah began to understand that God's saving work for his people Israel was intended to be known and experienced by all the people of the world. The "glory of the Lord" is the manifestation of God's presence and saving power. The return of the people of Judah across a desert highway, revealing the Lord's glory, will be a witness to all people of the salvation offered through the God of Israel.

In the New Testament, the writer of the letter to the Hebrews calls Jesus "the reflection of God's glory" (Heb 1:3). The full revelation of God's glory to all humanity is accomplished in the Messiah's coming. He will redeem God's people from a bondage far more profound than the captivity of Babylon. Through the saving work of the Messiah, all humanity is offered the truest freedom and the fullness of everlasting life.

Reflection and discussion

- Why does Handel introduce *Messiah* with the words of a prophet who lived five centuries before Christ? In what ways is Isaiah reinterpreted for this new context?

- Why were the tender words of Isaiah so comforting for God's people? Which words of Isaiah are most comforting to me?

- What obstacles need to be removed for me to experience the work of the Messiah in my life? What needs to be raised, lowered, straightened, or smoothed?

- How do the words and music of the chorus instill confidence in God within me?

Prayer

Tender and compassionate God, you have heard the cries of your people and have come to rescue them from bondage. Help me to prepare for the coming of your Messiah so that my life may be a witness of your glory for all to see.

The latter splendor of this house shall be greater than the former, says the Lord of hosts; and in this place I will give prosperity, says the Lord of hosts. HAGGAI 2:9

The Future Glory of God's Temple

5. RECITATIVE (Bass)

Thus saith the Lord of hosts: Yet once a little while and I will shake the heavens and the earth, the sea and the dry land; and I will shake all nations; and the desire of all nations shall come. The Lord, whom you seek, shall suddenly come to His temple, even the messenger of the covenant, whom ye delight in; behold, He shall come, saith the Lord of hosts. (Haggai 2:6, 7; Malachi 3:1)

HAGGAI 2:1–9 [1]*In the second year of King Darius, in the seventh month, on the
twenty-first day of the month, the word of the Lord came by the prophet Haggai,
saying:* [2]*Speak now to Zerubbabel son of Shealtiel, governor of Judah, and to
Joshua son of Jehozadak, the high priest, and to the remnant of the people, and
say,* [3]*Who is left among you that saw this house in its former glory? How does
it look to you now? Is it not in your sight as nothing?* [4]*Yet now take courage, O
Zerubbabel, says the Lord; take courage, O Joshua, son of Jehozadak, the high
priest; take courage, all you people of the land, says the Lord; work, for I am with
you, says the Lord of hosts,* [5]*according to the promise that I made you when you
came out of Egypt. My spirit abides among you; do not fear.* [6]*For thus says the
Lord of hosts: Once again, in a little while, I will shake the heavens and the earth*

and the sea and the dry land; [7]and I will shake all the nations, so that the treasure of all nations shall come, and I will fill this house with splendor, says the Lord of hosts. [8]The silver is mine, and the gold is mine, says the Lord of hosts. [9]The latter splendor of this house shall be greater than the former, says the Lord of hosts; and in this place I will give prosperity, says the Lord of hosts.

The revelation of God's glory to all people (Isaiah 40:5) will not only be a time of comfort, as Isaiah proclaimed, but also a challenging time of upheaval. The coming of the Messiah is a moment of both salvation and judgment, so the prophetic message is one of both joyful anticipation and attentive warning. The bass soloist conveys this ominous character of the Messiah's advent with a menacing rhythm.

Handel again expresses the poetic images of the prophet's text with tone painting, shaping the vocal music according to the meaning of the words. The musical line quakes and trembles on the word "shake" to communicate the monumental significance of this revelation of God's glory. The music again reverberates on the word "desire," revealing that the "desire of all nations" is the Messiah whose coming will shake the heavens and the earth.

Five centuries before the coming of Christ, the Jewish exiles were freed from Babylon by King Cyrus of Persia and returned to Jerusalem. But they discovered that the anticipation of their homecoming was more exhilarating than the reality. What they found there was a depopulated city, a depressed economy, broken city walls, and a ruined temple. They realized that they would not only need to rebuild their society, but in order to reclaim their religious heritage, they would have to rebuild the temple and purify their worship.

But how can human hands build a house worthy of the Lord's glory? A few of those who returned to Jerusalem remembered the temple of Solomon in its former glory (verse 3). But even Solomon himself prayed to the Lord of glory: "But will God indeed dwell on the earth? Even heaven and the highest heaven cannot contain you, much less this house that I have built!" (1 Kings 8:27). An earthly temple can never adequately contain the presence of the living God. Those who mourned the loss of the former temple had forgotten that it was not Solomon but God who filled that temple with divine glory.

Those who trust in the God of the past and the future must realize that God can manifest his glory in ways not yet imagined.

The prophet Haggai spoke God's word of encouragement to the people of Jerusalem: "Take courage. I am with you. My spirit abides among you. Do not fear" (verses 4–5). God will "shake" the cosmos and all the nations, and "the treasure of all nations" will come to "fill this house with splendor" (verse 7). Just as God shook the earth when he brought his people out of Egypt and revealed his covenant on Mount Sinai, the quaking land and sea poetically describes the disturbing revelation of God's glory. In fact, the magnificence of God's future temple will exceed that of Solomon's temple: "The latter splendor of this house shall be greater than the former" (verse 9).

This hopeful promise remained unfulfilled in the days of Haggai. The rebuilt temple was a poor reflection of its former splendor. Yet, the faithful God of Israel's covenant always offers great expectations for his people's future. When the Messiah came to the temple in Jerusalem, he cleansed it in judgment and predicted its destruction. Yet, he himself is the revelation of God's glory, the temple not made with human hands (Mark 14:58), the temple that will be destroyed and raised again in three days (John 2:19–21).

Reflection and discussion

- What is Handel expressing by the trembling musical line on the word "shake" and "desire"?

- In what sense does this scene express the Lord's coming from a contrasting point of view?

- In what way is the latter splendor of the temple greater than the former splendor of Solomon's temple?

- How does the prophet Haggai prepare us for the temple ministry of Jesus in the gospels?

- Which words of Haggai offer me the most hope and confidence for the future?

Prayer

Mighty God, the heavens and the earth tremble at your presence, though you offer encouragement and hope to your people. Fill me with expectations for whatever future you have in store for me and help me place my trust in you.

Ever since the days of your ancestors you have turned aside from my statutes and have not kept them. Return to me, and I will return to you, says the Lord of hosts. MALACHI 3:7

Like a Refiner's Fire

6. ARIA (Bass, Tenor, Alto, or Soprano)
But who may abide the day of His coming, and who shall stand when He appeareth? For He is like a refiner's fire. (Malachi 3:2)

7. CHORUS
And He shall purify the sons of Levi, that they may offer unto the Lord an offering in righteousness. (Malachi 3:3)

MALACHI 3:1–7 [1]*See, I am sending my messenger to prepare the way before me,*
and the Lord whom you seek will suddenly come to his temple. The messenger of
the covenant in whom you delight—indeed, he is coming, says the Lord of hosts.
[2]*But who can endure the day of his coming, and who can stand when he appears?*
For he is like a refiner's fire and like fullers' soap; [3]*he will sit as a refiner and*
purifier of silver, and he will purify the descendants of Levi and refine them like
gold and silver, until they present offerings to the Lord in righteousness. [4]*Then the*
offering of Judah and Jerusalem will be pleasing to the Lord as in the days of old
and as in former years.

[5]*Then I will draw near to you for judgment; I will be swift to bear witness against*
the sorcerers, against the adulterers, against those who swear falsely, against those
who oppress the hired workers in their wages, the widow and the orphan, against
those who thrust aside the alien, and do not fear me, says the Lord of hosts.

[6]For I the Lord do not change; therefore you, O children of Jacob, have not perished. [7]Ever since the days of your ancestors you have turned aside from my statutes and have not kept them. Return to me, and I will return to you, says the Lord of hosts.

Messiah encourages two complementary responses to the revelation of God's glory on earth: tender comfort and reverential awe. While it is wonderful to think that the Lord will suddenly come to his temple (verse 1), it is also a sobering thought. Handel's aria asks how people will be able to survive the experience of his coming: "Who can endure the day of his coming, and who can stand when he appears?" (verse 2). The question is asked in a melodic voice which then breaks into ferocious embellishment when describing the Lord's presence: "For he is like a refiner's fire." The notes of the aria create a sense in which the words "refiner's fire" seem to glow with intense heat and leap up with raging melismas like hot flames.

Though the Lord's coming is a frightening prospect, his purpose is the purification of his people. He is like the intensely hot fire of a refiner which heats gold and silver until all the dross and impurities are burned away. In the fire, the metal is refined so all that is left is pure gold or pure silver. The full prophetic text also compares the Lord to "fullers' soap" (verse 2), the bleaching agent used in the laundries of the ancient world. Both images emphasize that the Lord's coming is a cleansing event, making it possible for sinful people to stand before an awesome God.

The chorus emphasizes this process of purification. The word "purify" is embellished with coloratura, and the entire movement is sung with a pure and gentle voice in stark contrast to the fierce intensity of "refiner's fire." The chorus expresses the people's hope of being cleansed and rendered worthy to come before the Lord.

For ancient Israel at the time of the prophet Malachi, this process of repentance and cleansing had to begin in the temple with those charged with offering sacrifice for the forgiveness of the people's sins. The "descendants of Levi" were the priests of Israel, charged with carrying out the offerings and functions of the temple (verse 3). The prophet accuses these priests of faithlessness and much corruption (Mal 2:1–9). When they have been purified, they will "present offerings to the Lord in righteousness," offering sacrifices with clean hands and pure hearts that are "pleasing to the Lord as in the days of old" (verse 4).

The New Testament presents the Messiah as the priest of God's people. The letter to the Hebrews declares that Jesus is the faithful high priest whose sacrifice on our behalf is eternally pleasing to God. His one sacrifice was an offering of atonement for the sins of all people (Heb 2:17). It is this sacrifice of the Messiah which will finally purify all God's people and present our lives in union with Christ's as a worthy offering to God.

In the days of the prophet Malachi, even though the Jews had returned to Jerusalem and rebuilt the temple, they disregarded God's commands and questioned God's relationship with them in covenant. But Malachi warned the people that "the messenger of the covenant" is coming, a frightening prospect for those who need to be refined and purified. The Lord will come in judgment against evildoers and all who oppress those in need (verse 5). But God does not cause his sinful people to perish (verse 6); rather, he urges them to be distilled and cleansed. He remains the God of the covenant; as he said, "I the Lord do not change." God continues to use Israel as his instrument to bring his reign of justice and peace to all the people of the earth. So he comes to his people as a refining fire, a purifying flame. God's message is clear: "Return to me, and I will return to you, says the Lord of hosts" (verse 7).

Reflection and discussion

- Which emotions are most important to experience in preparation for the coming of the Messiah? Comfort, reverence, affection, repentance? On which do I need to focus?

- What evidence do I have that God has put me through a refiner's fire and refused to give up on me? In what ways has my faith been tested and purified (see 1 Peter 1:7)?

- Why do I need to be cleansed and rendered worthy to come before the Lord?

- In what way is the Messiah also our high priest? How does the offering of our lives become acceptable and pleasing to God?

Prayer

Lord of the Covenant, you are faithful to your promises even when your people turn away from you. Give me a spirit of repentance so that I may return to you. Purify me with a refiner's fire so that the offering of my life will be pleasing to you.

Then Isaiah said: "Hear then, O house of David! Is it too little for you to weary mortals, that you weary my God also? Therefore the Lord himself will give you a sign." ISAIAH 7:13–14

Emmanuel, God with Us

8. RECITATIVE (Alto)

Behold, a virgin shall conceive and bear a son, and shall call His name Emmanuel, God with us. (Isaiah 7:14; Matthew 1:23)

ISAIAH 7:10–17 [10]*Again the Lord spoke to Ahaz, saying,* [11]*Ask a sign of the Lord your God; let it be deep as Sheol or high as heaven.* [12]*But Ahaz said, I will not ask, and I will not put the Lord to the test.* [13]*Then Isaiah said: "Hear then, O house of David! Is it too little for you to weary mortals, that you weary my God also?* [14]*Therefore the Lord himself will give you a sign. Look, the young woman is with child and shall bear a son, and shall name him Immanuel.* [15]*He shall eat curds and honey by the time he knows how to refuse the evil and choose the good.* [16]*For before the child knows how to refuse the evil and choose the good, the land before whose two kings you are in dread will be deserted.* [17]*The Lord will bring on you and on your people and on your ancestral house such days as have not come since the day that Ephraim departed from Judah—the king of Assyria."*

MATTHEW 1:18–25 [18]*Now the birth of Jesus the Messiah took place in this way. When his mother Mary had been engaged to Joseph, but before they lived together, she was found to be with child from the Holy Spirit.* [19]*Her husband Joseph, being a*

righteous man and unwilling to expose her to public disgrace, planned to dismiss her
quietly. [20]But just when he had resolved to do this, an angel of the Lord appeared to
him in a dream and said, "Joseph, son of David, do not be afraid to take Mary as
your wife, for the child conceived in her is from the Holy Spirit. [21]She will bear a son,
and you are to name him Jesus, for he will save his people from their sins." [22]All this
took place to fulfill what had been spoken by the Lord through the prophet:
[23]"Look, the virgin shall conceive and bear a son,
and they shall name him Emmanuel,"
which means, "God is with us." [24]When Joseph awoke from sleep, he did as the
angel of the Lord commanded him; he took her as his wife, [25]but had no marital
relations with her until she had borne a son; and he named him Jesus.

This first alto solo is sparse and unadorned. It announces the birth of the Messiah with the timeless words of the ancient prophet Isaiah. Like the dark and dangerous period in which Isaiah prophesied, the time of Jesus' birth was a threatening period for the Jewish people. But when all seems dark and hope seems lost, the God of saving grace hears the longing cries of his people. The birth of the child who will be called Emmanuel is the promise of God's presence with his people. In Handel's original manuscript of *Messiah*, now displayed in the British Museum, the words "God with us" are written in letters fully twice the size of the preceding words. In performance, these final words are proceeded by a pause, just long enough to heighten the listener's expectation. Truly the coming of the Messiah is the definitive sign of "God with us."

The prophetic writings of the Old Testament are multilayered in their meaning, and their truth cannot be contained in one moment in history. God's people continue to find meaning in the prophetic writings in new contexts. When Isaiah spoke of the child to be named Emmanuel, he was not consciously thinking of the birth of a child centuries later in Bethlehem. Rather, he was addressing Ahaz, the king reigning in Jerusalem in the eighth century before Christ. The king's enemies were forming an alliance and planning to renew their assault on Jerusalem.

When Isaiah assured Ahaz that God would prevail, the king found it difficult to believe. Challenged by God's prophet to radical faith, the king was only capable of fear. So, God offered Ahaz a sign that his promises could be trusted (Isaiah 7:14). The sign was the birth of a child from a young maiden, probably meant to foretell the birth of a new king. This child was to be a physical reassertion that God is present with his people as guardian and protector. He is named Emmanuel, God-with-us, so God's people need not be afraid.

Matthew chose this ancient prophecy to mark the beginning of the Christian story (Matt 1:23). The text he used was the Greek version of Isaiah, specifying that the mother of the child was a virgin. Isaiah's prophecy, in this new context, spoke of a child through whom God's people would experience the presence of God. God himself would live with his people in a way that is both humanly ordinary and divinely miraculous—coming as a tiny child born to a virgin mother.

Out of the doubts and fears of God's ancient people came this remarkable prophecy of the Messiah's birth. He will be God-with-us, not in a way that anyone could have predicted—not coming on the clouds with hosts of angels, not appearing on a mountain amid fire and quaking, not wielding a sword of chastisement and justice—but God-with-us in a Bethlehem stable, vulnerable to every indignity of human experience. Yet, this tiny baby will be born of his virgin mother and be called Son of the Most High. God will give him the throne of his ancestor King David and his reign will never end.

Reflection and discussion

- In what way can this text be described as multilayered in its meaning?

- Why does the alto voice speak the mystery of Christ's birth in such a subdued and unadorned way?

- How does Matthew use this text of Isaiah in a new context to tell of the birth of Jesus?

- How does Matthew's use of Isaiah's prophecy indicate that the birth of Jesus is both humanly ordinary and divinely miraculous?

- In what way have I experienced a lack of trust like that of Ahaz? How does this text assure me of God's presence in the midst of life's doubts and fears?

Prayer

Guardian of ancient Israel, you respond with your saving grace when all seems dark and when I am fearful. Renew my trust in your promises and help me believe that you are with me in the best and worst of times.

Lift up your eyes and look around; they all gather together, they come to you; your sons shall come from far away, and your daughters shall be carried on their nurses' arms. ISAIAH 60:4

God's Glory Shines in the Darkness

9. ARIA (Alto) AND CHORUS

O thou that tellest good tidings to Zion, get thee up into the high mountain. O though that tellest good tidings to Jerusalem, lift up thy voice with strength; lift it up, be not afraid, say unto the cities of Judah: Behold your God! Arise, shine, for thy light is come, and the glory of the Lord is risen upon thee. (Isaiah 40:9; 60:1)

10. RECITATIVE (Bass)

For behold, darkness shall cover the earth, and gross darkness the people; but the Lord shall arise upon thee, and His glory shall be seen upon thee, and the Gentiles shall come to thy light, and kings to the brightness of thy rising. (Isaiah 60:2, 3)

ISAIAH 40:9

9 *Get you up to a high mountain,*
O Zion, herald of good tidings;
lift up your voice with strength,
O Jerusalem, herald of good tidings,
lift it up, do not fear;

say to the cities of Judah,
"Here is your God!"

ISAIAH 60:1–6

1 *Arise, shine; for your light has come,*
and the glory of the Lord has risen upon you.
2 *For darkness shall cover the earth,*
and thick darkness the peoples;
but the Lord will arise upon you,
and his glory will appear over you.
3 *Nations shall come to your light,*
and kings to the brightness of your dawn.

4 *Lift up your eyes and look around;*
they all gather together, they come to you;
your sons shall come from far away,
and your daughters shall be carried on their nurses' arms.
5 *Then you shall see and be radiant;*
your heart shall thrill and rejoice,
because the abundance of the sea shall be brought to you,
the wealth of the nations shall come to you.
6 *A multitude of camels shall cover you,*
the young camels of Midian and Ephah;
all those from Sheba shall come.
They shall bring gold and frankincense,
and shall proclaim the praise of the Lord.

Handel's oratorio continues to proclaim passages from Isaiah which the church has used to express the meaning of Christ's coming to the world. Following the simple and subdued recitative announcing the birth of Emmanuel, the alto aria proclaims the meaning of that announcement with uplifted joy. The ascending melody musically manifests the "high mountain" from which the "good tidings" are proclaimed (40:9). The phrases "lift up thy voice with strength, lift it up, be not afraid" lead to the bold proclamation "Behold your God!" The aria continues with the melody rising still higher, expressing the shining light of God's glory. Without a pause, the chorus then echoes the joyful enthusiasm of the bearer of good tidings and the joy of God's people upon whom the glorious light has risen.

Isaiah's prophecy proclaimed the good tidings that a new day has arisen for those held in the exile of Babylon. God is leading his people home again to Jerusalem. The good news is something to shout and sing about. Indeed, the glory of the Lord was coming up over the mountain like the dawn of a new day.

Handel uses these Advent images of Isaiah to proclaim the joyful news that God has come to save his captive people through Jesus, the Messiah. His coming is the good tidings proclaimed to God's people. He is the light of God's glory. He is the definitive presence of God in the midst of God's people. There are no tidings more joyful, no news more wonderful.

The bass recitative expresses the contrast between the heavy darkness in which God's people formerly walked and the brilliant light that has dawned upon them (60:2). The music paints a gloomy and somber condition, and then it slowly rises to convey the emerging light. The words "arise" and "glory" receive special musical emphasis with melismas. The bass voice "arises" from the murky depths and sings of the Lord's "glory" that will shine for all the nations to see.

Jesus is the true light for all people. As John's Gospel proclaims, "The true light, which enlightens everyone, was coming into the world" (John 1:9). When the whole world is enshrouded in darkness, the Messiah comes as light not only to Israel but to all peoples of the earth. Gentiles and kings will come to "the brightness" of his rising (60:3). The light that shines on Jerusalem has come to illuminate the whole world.

The early Christians understood that the first manifestation of Isaiah's prophecy was seen in the magi from the East who visited the newborn Messiah. This text of Isaiah is the origin of the tradition that the magi were Gentile kings who brought their gifts to the infant Jesus. They followed the bright, shining star at his birth, the first representatives of all the earth's people who will be drawn by his light. Even the well-known tradition that the magi traveled by camel is rooted in the words of the ancient prophet (60:6). Both the words of Isaiah and the journey of the magi point to the universality of God's salvation revealed in the dawning light of Christ.

Reflection and discussion

- Why am I often afraid to lift up my voice and tell the good tidings of God's presence in my life? What good news do I readily share?

- Why does the world so often prefer the darkness to the light? Where do I need to shine some light?

- Why do the opening and closing verses of the Bible offer us images of light (Gen 1:3; Rev 22:5)? Why is light such a powerful metaphor of God's presence?

Prayer

God of all nations, your light has shown upon your people in the darkness of captivity. In your Messiah you have illumined the world with the light of your glory. May I be unafraid to lift up my voice and sing the good tidings of your coming among us.

SUGGESTIONS FOR FACILITATORS, GROUP SESSION 2

1. If there are newcomers who were not present for the first group session, introduce them now.

2. You may want to pray this prayer as a group:
   Guardian of ancient Israel and Lord of all nations, you are faithful to your promises even when we turn away from you. Purify our hearts with the fire of your love so that the offering of our lives will be pleasing to you. Stir up hope within us and give us confidence in your redeeming power, even when all looks dark and our fears seem overwhelming. Fill us with expectation for the future you have in store for us and help us place our confidence in you. As you renew us with your inspired word, make us witnesses of your glory for all to see.

3. Ask one or both of the following questions:
   - What was your biggest challenge in Bible study over this past week?
   - What did you learn about yourself this week?

4. Discuss lessons 1 through 6 together. Assuming that group members have read the Scripture and commentary during the week, there is no need to read it aloud. As you review each lesson, you might want to briefly summarize the Scripture passages of each lesson and ask the group what stands out most clearly from the commentary.

5. Choose one or more of the questions for reflection and discussion from each lesson to talk over as a group. You may want to ask group members which question was most challenging or helpful to them as you review each lesson.

6. Keep the discussion moving, but don't rush it in order to complete more questions. Allow time for the questions that provoke the best discussion.

7. Instruct group members to complete lessons 7 through 12 on their own during the six days before the next group meeting. They should write out their own answers to the questions as preparation for next week's group discussion.

8. Conclude by praying aloud together the prayer at the end of lesson 6 or any other prayer you choose.

His authority shall grow continually, and there shall be endless peace for the throne of David and his kingdom. He will establish and uphold it with justice and with righteousness. ISAIAH 9:7

Unto Us a Child Is Born

11. ARIA (Bass)

The people that walked in darkness have seen a great light; and they that dwell in the land of the shadow of death, upon them hath the light shined. (Isaiah 9:2)

12. CHORUS

For unto us a child is born, unto us a son is given, and the government shall be upon His shoulder; and His name shall be called Wonderful, Counsellor, The Mighty God, The Everlasting Father, The Prince of Peace. (Isaiah 9:6)

ISAIAH 9:1–7 1*But there will be no gloom for those who were in anguish. In the former time he brought into contempt the land of Zebulun and the land of Naphtali, but in the latter time he will make glorious the way of the sea, the land beyond the Jordan, Galilee of the nations.*

2*The people who walked in darkness*
have seen a great light;
those who lived in a land of deep darkness—
on them light has shined.
3*You have multiplied the nation,*
you have increased its joy;

they rejoice before you
as with joy at the harvest,
as people exult when dividing plunder.
[4]*For the yoke of their burden,*
and the bar across their shoulders,
the rod of their oppressor,
you have broken as on the day of Midian.
[5]*For all the boots of the tramping warriors*
and all the garments rolled in blood
shall be burned as fuel for the fire.
[6]*For a child has been born for us,*
a son given to us;
authority rests upon his shoulders;
and he is named
Wonderful Counselor, Mighty God,
Everlasting Father, Prince of Peace.
[7]*His authority shall grow continually,*
and there shall be endless peace
for the throne of David and his kingdom.
He will establish and uphold it
with justice and with righteousness
from this time onward and forevermore.
The zeal of the Lord of hosts will do this.

The bass aria continues to express the contrast of light and darkness fashioned by the ancient prophet Isaiah. The voice and strings express the aimless and meandering stride of "the people that walked in darkness." But for those wandering in "the land of the shadow of death," God's blessing has come. The wondrous light has been seen and sheds its radiance into the darkness, yet its shining brightness has not yet broken forth into full glory.

Then, the first climax of *Messiah* arrives as the chorus sings the beloved "For unto us a child is born." Hope is fulfilled; the wonder has taken place. All God's people sing together in joy over the birth of the royal child. The prophecies of Isaiah have been building up to this moment, representing the Messiah's birth and the dawning of salvation. The melody with its birth announcement is introduced first by the delicate soprano voices, then the tenors and other voices join in contrapuntal enthusiasm until all voices blend together to jubilantly proclaim the royal titles: "Wonderful, Counsellor, the mighty God, the everlasting Father, the Prince of Peace."

These words of Isaiah express a decisive change in the fortunes of Judah. The "former time" (verse 1) is the period of conquest and subjugation; the "latter time" is a period of new royal leadership in the line of David. Through a new king, God is coming into the lives of his people and creating a wondrous new possibility. The darkness is transformed into a splendid light (verse 2), and the gloom is overcome by great joy (verse 3). The yoke and the rod of oppression are broken (verse 4) by the one who has the authority to reverse the fortunes of his people.

The royal child is given titles indicating his sharing in divine rule and power (verse 6). "Wonderful Counselor" designates one who devises wise plans and is able to carry them out. "Mighty God" designates a king who shares in God's power to do whatever is necessary for the salvation of his people. "Everlasting Father" emphasizes his faithful, devoted care for the people. "Prince of Peace" expresses the peacemaking qualities of the king who would bring completeness and harmony to the kingdom under his reign.

As the wondrous period announced by Isaiah failed to come about in ancient times, the people of Judah began to understand these passages as messianic texts, referring to a future king who would rule with justice, righteousness, and peace forevermore (verse 7). The Messiah from the line of David would be king and savior of his people par excellence. Though Isaiah himself was not peering into the distant future to predict the birth of Jesus, he knew that the hope contained in these texts would survive even the loss of the kingship in his people's exile. Whenever the Jewish people looked for divine deliverance from oppression, they turned to the hope instilled in these texts. When Jesus came into the world, his Jewish disciples knew that he was the final fulfillment of their hope.

Reflection and discussion

- What experience in my life has divided the "former time" and the "latter time"? How was God involved in that transition?

- Which of Isaiah's messianic titles (verse 6) best expresses my understanding of Christ?

- How does Matthew's gospel reinterpret this text of Isaiah (Matthew 4:12–16)?

Prayer

Wonderful Counselor, fill my darkness with the light of your wisdom and hope. Prince of Peace, banish the gloom of hatred and strife and bring the justice of your reign upon the earth. Come, Lord Jesus.

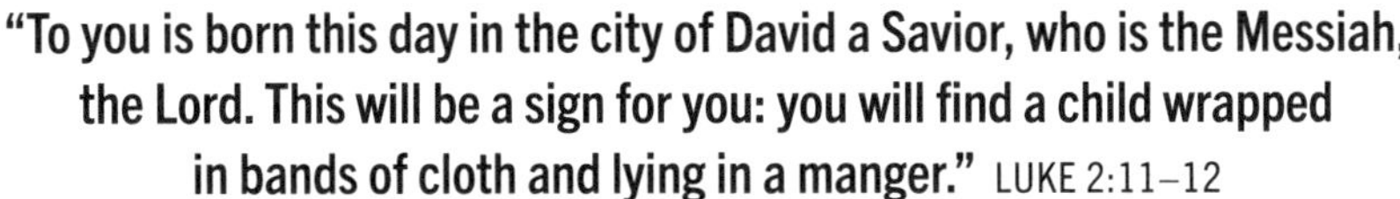
"To you is born this day in the city of David a Savior, who is the Messiah, the Lord. This will be a sign for you: you will find a child wrapped in bands of cloth and lying in a manger." LUKE 2:11–12

The Message of the Lord's Angel

13. PIFA – PASTORAL SYMPHONY (Orchestra)

14. RECITATIVE (Soprano)

There were shepherds abiding in the fields, keeping watch over their flock by night. (Luke 2:8)

And lo, the angel of the Lord came upon them, and the glory of the Lord shone round about them, and they were sore afraid. (Luke 2:9)

15. RECITATIVE (Soprano)

And the angel said unto them: Fear not; for behold, I bring you tidings of great joy, which shall be to all people; for unto you is born this day in the city of David a Saviour, which is Christ the Lord. (Luke 2:10, 11)

LUKE 2:8–12 8*In that region there were shepherds living in the fields, keeping*
watch over their flock by night. 9*Then an angel of the Lord stood before them, and*
the glory of the Lord shone around them, and they were terrified. 10*But the angel*
said to them, "Do not be afraid; for see—I am bringing you good news of great joy
for all the people: 11*to you is born this day in the city of David a Savior, who is the*
Messiah, the Lord. 12*This will be a sign for you: you will find a child wrapped in*
bands of cloth and lying in a manger."

Messiah's voices pause after the Old Testament prophetic texts for an instrumental work which introduces the angel's announcement of the Messiah's birth. The gentle, lyrical "pastoral symphony" relaxes us among the shepherds on the quiet hillsides near Bethlehem, only to be interrupted by the startling declaration of the angel. The soprano voice is serene as she narrates the story of the shepherds living in the fields, keeping the night watch over their flock. Her voice then stirs with exhilaration as she tells of the appearance of the angel and the fear of the shepherds.

The announcement of Christ's birth is made on a remote hillside to simple shepherds. Holding no social or religious status in Israel, the shepherds were lowly people of the land. With the mention of the shepherds, Handel's audience probably thought of the idyllic pastoral scenes of English literature. But the shepherds of Israel were hardworking people who lived in the fields, leading their flock by day and sleeping with the sheep at night. As the angel appeared to them, and God's glory shone upon them, "they were terrified" (verse 9).

The appearance of an angel in biblical texts is never an idyllic scene, filled with charming sweetness. Fear is the typical response of one who encounters a messenger of the Lord in the stories of Scripture. Yet, the message of God to one who experiences such a divine encounter is always one of comforting reassurance: "Do not be afraid" (verse 10). In Luke's account, the angel of God proclaims "good news of great joy for all the people." This word from God counteracts the great fear of the shepherds with the great joy of the message.

The soprano recitative again becomes hushed as the announcement is made. Accompanied by only a few chords, the soprano makes known the good news as the world listens breathlessly. The angel sums up the entire message of the gospel by announcing that the child born in Bethlehem is Savior, Messiah, and Lord (verse 11). As Savior, Jesus will rescue humanity from sin and heal the divisions that separate people from God and from one another. As Messiah (or Christ), Jesus is the anointed heir of David, the one who will establish God's kingdom. As Lord, Jesus is proclaimed with the same divine title used of God in the Old Testament, and he is invested with divine authority.

A baby "wrapped in bands of cloth and lying in a manger" (verse 12) is not the kind of "sign" we might expect at the birth of one who is Savior, Messiah, and Lord. The simplicity of the sign and the lowliness of those who first heard the message contrasts with the regal identity of the child that the angel just proclaimed. The angel invites the shepherds and all the hearers of the gospel to contemplate both the humility and the majesty of this newborn king. Because he did not choose wealth and power, we can come to him ragtag and unembarrassed. Because he became like us, we can become like him.

Reflection and discussion

- Of all the people of the world the angels could have visited, why would God want the Messiah's birth first announced to shepherds?

- In what way does the good news borne by the angels summarize the whole message of the gospel?

- In what ways does the music indicate both the simplicity and the magnificence of the event it proclaims?

Prayer

Savior, Messiah, and Lord, you were presented to the world in a lowly manger and announced to humble shepherds. Help me to contemplate the mystery of your simple beginnings and to be a herald of this good news of great joy.

When the angels had left them and gone into heaven, the shepherds said to one another, "Let us go now to Bethlehem and see this thing that has taken place, which the Lord has made known to us." LUKE 2:15

The Angels and Shepherds Glorify God

16. RECITATIVE (Soprano)
And suddenly there was with the angel a multitude of the heavenly host praising God, and saying: (Luke 2:13)

17. CHORUS
Glory to God in the highest, and peace on earth, good will toward men. (Luke 2:14)

LUKE 2:13–20 13*And suddenly there was with the angel a multitude of the heav-*
enly host, praising God and saying,
14*"Glory to God in the highest heaven,*
and on earth peace among those whom he favors!"
15*When the angels had left them and gone into heaven, the shepherds said to*
one another, "Let us go now to Bethlehem and see this thing that has taken place,
which the Lord has made known to us." 16*So they went with haste and found Mary*
and Joseph, and the child lying in the manger. 17*When they saw this, they made*
known what had been told them about this child; 18*and all who heard it were*
amazed at what the shepherds told them. 19*But Mary treasured all these words*
and pondered them in her heart. 20*The shepherds returned, glorifying and praising*
God for all they had heard and seen, as it had been told them.

The brief recitative is directly linked to the chorus, declaring the response of the heavenly creatures to the marvelous announcement of the Messiah's birth. In the "Glory to God" chorus, Handel uses trumpets for the first time. Yet, clearly he does not want a deafening "Glory." He indicates that the trumpets are to be played "at a distance and quietly." The sound of the chorus builds in an eruption of praise, as if the glory were pouring down from heaven to the streets and fields of the earth. Still, at the end, the angels seem to leave even less obtrusively than they came. The orchestration becomes thinner and the dynamics are reduced to "very quiet" at the conclusion of the chorus, as the angels leave the shepherds and return in flight to the heavens.

The angels declare the significance of the birth of Jesus from two sides: the heavenly and the earthly (verse 14). The birth of the Messiah is the supreme event in human history by which God is glorified, and that same event offers peace for those on the earth. This two-tiered significance of Christ's birth is effectively expressed by the voices of the chorus. The glory in the heavens, sung by the soprano voices accompanied by the high violins, is contrasted with "peace on earth," sung by bass voices accompanied by low strings. In Christ's wondrous birth, God in heaven is given glory; people on earth are brought peace.

"Peace" in the Hebrew understanding, expressed by the word *shalom*, means "wholeness" and "completeness." This peace is more than just the absence of war and hostility. In the writings of the later prophets, peace was a primary characteristic of the messianic age to come. The Messiah would be the Prince of Peace. Human sin and evil took away the wholeness that God wishes his people to experience, but the coming of Christ offers humanity again the possibility of restoring that lost completeness. The one who will save his people from their sins will heal their wounds and make them whole again.

The canticle of the angels, the Gloria (verse 14), may have been a refrain sung by the early Christians in their worship. The church's liturgy has continued to include this song of the angels in its introductory rites. With confidence in the revelation of Jesus as Savior, Messiah, and Lord, God's people can join with the heavenly hosts in praising God for this great manifestation of his goodness to humanity.

Reflection and discussion

- In what ways do the voices and musical dynamics of the chorus express the complementary effects of Christ's birth for both heaven and earth?

- In what ways does the coming of the Messiah offer glory to God and peace to humanity?

- How does Jesus offer a peace that the world cannot give? In what ways do I experience the *shalom* that God desires for me?

Prayer

Prince of Peace, come upon the earth with your power to heal and forgive. Heal the wounds that sin has caused among your people and reconcile your people to God so that we may always give glory to God in the highest.

He will cut off the chariot from Ephraim and the war-horse from Jerusalem; and the battle bow shall be cut off, and he shall command peace to the nations; his dominion shall be from sea to sea, and from the River to the ends of the earth. ZECHARIAH 9:10

Behold the King Who Speaks Peace

18. ARIA (Soprano)

Rejoice greatly, O daughter of Zion! Shout, O daughter of Jerusalem! Behold, thy King cometh unto thee! He is the righteous Saviour, and He shall speak peace unto the heathen. (Zechariah 9:9, 10)

ZECHARIAH 9:8–10

8 *Then I will encamp at my house as a guard,*
so that no one shall march to and fro;
no oppressor shall again overrun them,
for now I have seen with my own eyes.

9 *Rejoice greatly, O daughter Zion!*
Shout aloud, O daughter Jerusalem!
Lo, your king comes to you;
triumphant and victorious is he,
humble and riding on a donkey,
on a colt, the foal of a donkey.
10 *He will cut off the chariot from Ephraim*
and the war-horse from Jerusalem;

and the battle bow shall be cut off,
and he shall command peace to the nations;
his dominion shall be from sea to sea,
and from the River to the ends of the earth.

In this jubilant aria, the soprano announces the coming of the messianic king to his city, Jerusalem. The word "rejoice" is particularly embellished and sung with exuberant joy. Through the words of the prophet, the singer calls on "daughter Zion," "daughter Jerusalem," to go out and meet the newly crowned or newly triumphant king. Carrying branches and garlands, the people of the city "rejoice greatly" with psalms of praise and "shout aloud" with cries of triumph.

Zechariah tells of God's protection for the people of Jerusalem because God is standing guard over his people at his own house, the city's temple (verse 8). He then announces the royal Messiah's coming to govern the kingdom of God (verse 9). He is a "righteous Saviour" of his people, ruling them as a just king over his subjects.

The two prominent characteristics of the Messiah's reign are its peacefulness and its universality. Chariots, war-horses, and battle bows will be done away with, and "he shall command peace to the nations" (verse10). ("Heathen" is an archaic word for Gentiles or people of other lands who do not acknowledge the God of Israel.) The Messiah's dominion will extend from its center in Jerusalem to the entire known world, "from sea to sea, from the river to the ends of the earth." The blessings of divine *shalom* will prevail wherever the Messiah rules.

When Jesus entered the city of Jerusalem, he came riding on a donkey. The evangelists quote these words of Zechariah to describe Christ's peaceful and humble entry into his own city. He comes humbly, not riding above the heads of his people on a warhorse or swiftly on a chariot, but on a pure-bred ass. He will certainly triumph and bring his reign of peace. Yet, his humble character makes a profound statement about the nature of genuine authority and power. He will prevail not by assembling conquering armies but by subverting his foes through pastoral service and sacrificial love.

The writers of the gospels show that this prophecy of Zechariah is a witness to the messianic identity of Jesus and a joyful announcement that our Messiah has now come to us. The movements of *Messiah* which follow reflect on the earthly character of the humble Savior and our invitation to respond to him.

Reflection and discussion

- How does the aria's call to "rejoice" and "shout" make me feel? Does the Messiah's coming provoke exuberant joy within me?

- In what ways does Jesus fulfill both the peaceable and universal qualities of the Messiah's reign?

- How does the text indicate the humble character of the Messiah? How does this challenge my understanding of real power?

Prayer

Savior and King, you come to your people as we rejoice and shout in jubilation. You come to save your people and bring us your kingdom of peace. Destroy the weapons of the nations and bring your universal reign throughout the earth.

Strengthen the weak hands, and make firm the feeble knees. Say to those who are of a fearful heart, "Be strong, do not fear! Here is your God." ISAIAH 35:3–4

A Messiah Who Heals and Makes Whole

19. RECITATIVE (Alto)

Then shall the eyes of the blind be opened, and the ears of the deaf unstopped; then shall the lame man leap as an hart, and the tongue of the dumb shall sing. (Isaiah 35:5, 6)

ISAIAH 35:1–7

1The wilderness and the dry land shall be glad,
the desert shall rejoice and blossom;
like the crocus 2it shall blossom abundantly,
and rejoice with joy and singing.
The glory of Lebanon shall be given to it,
the majesty of Carmel and Sharon.
They shall see the glory of the Lord,
the majesty of our God.

3Strengthen the weak hands,
and make firm the feeble knees.
4Say to those who are of a fearful heart,
"Be strong, do not fear!
Here is your God.
He will come with vengeance,

with terrible recompense.
He will come and save you."

5 *Then the eyes of the blind shall be opened,*
and the ears of the deaf unstopped;
6 *then the lame shall leap like a deer,*
and the tongue of the speechless sing for joy.
For waters shall break forth in the wilderness,
and streams in the desert;
7 *the burning sand shall become a pool,*
and the thirsty ground springs of water;
the haunt of jackals shall become a swamp,
the grass shall become reeds and rushes.

The brief alto recitative proclaims a concise excerpt from Isaiah's declaration of God's healing power. The passage chosen for the libretto emphasizes God's healing of human disabilities. The blind, deaf, lame, and mute are restored to the community, and their dysfunctions are healed. This prophetic passage is shown in the gospels to be fulfilled in the healing ministry of Jesus, an indicator that he is truly "the one who is to come." Where Jesus is present, "the blind receive their sight, the lame walk, the lepers are cleansed, the deaf hear, the dead are raised, the poor have good news brought to them" (Luke 7:22).

The healings of Jesus are one aspect of the total salvation Jesus came to bring to the world. Jesus desired to make people whole, to heal them from all that oppressed them, isolated them from others, and impeded their fullness of life. Jesus did not necessarily cure every person who came to him with physical needs, but he healed many as a sign that the time for salvation had come. His physical healing of people was one facet of his ministry of bringing wholeness to God's creation.

The text of Isaiah tells of a future time when all creation will be healed and restored. God will transform the natural world to its full beauty and generativity (verses 1–2). The wilderness, dry land, and desert will be made fertile, producing blossoms and fruit. The land itself will burst forth in rejoicing and singing praise to God. In place of the wilderness, desert, burning sand,

and thirsty ground, God will bring forth waters, streams, pools, and springs (verses 6–7).

Within this renewed creation, the prophet situates our healed humanity (verses 3–6). The "weak hands," "feeble knees," and "fearful hearts" do not need to fear because God's salvation is coming. Humanity fully alive and whole will not be simply restored to its former condition; rather, God exceeds all expectation. The lame don't just walk again; they will leap like a deer. Those who are mute will not just speak again; they will sing for joy.

God's people awaited a Messiah who would restore their political fortunes, but God sent a Messiah who would heal all creation and create a new wholeness within humanity. Again, God's word of comfort becomes a living reality through the salvation offered by God's Messiah.

Reflection and discussion

- In what sense is God's creation incomplete and in need of being restored to wholeness? In what sense am I incomplete and in need of the wholeness offered by God's grace?

- In what sense might the healing offered by Jesus be different from the cure brought about by a physician?

Prayer

Healing Savior, I know that I am incomplete without the experience of your saving presence. Heal my blindness to your truth, open my ears to the cry of your suffering people, and lift up my voice to give you thanks and praise.

I have other sheep that do not belong to this fold.
I must bring them also, and they will listen to my voice.
So there will be one flock, one shepherd. JOHN 10:16

The Shepherd Feeds and Carries His Flock

20. ARIA (Alto)

He shall feed his flock like a shepherd; and He shall gather the lambs with His arm, and carry them in His bosom, and gently lead those that are with young. (Isaiah 40:11)

ARIA (Soprano)

Come unto Him, all ye that labour and are heavy laden, and He will give you rest. Take His yoke upon you, and learn of Him, for He is meek and lowly of heart, and ye shall find rest unto your souls. (Matthew 11:28, 29)

21. CHORUS

His yoke is easy, and His burthen is light. (Matthew 11:30)

ISAIAH 40:10–11

[10]*See, the Lord God comes with might,*
and his arm rules for him;
his reward is with him,
and his recompense before him.
[11]*He will feed his flock like a shepherd;*

he will gather the lambs in his arms,
and carry them in his bosom,
and gently lead the mother sheep.

JOHN 10:11–18 [11]*"I am the good shepherd. The good shepherd lays down his life for the sheep.* [12]*The hired hand, who is not the shepherd and does not own the sheep, sees the wolf coming and leaves the sheep and runs away—and the wolf snatches them and scatters them.* [13]*The hired hand runs away because a hired hand does not care for the sheep.* [14]*I am the good shepherd. I know my own and my own know me,* [15]*just as the Father knows me and I know the Father. And I lay down my life for the sheep.* [16]*I have other sheep that do not belong to this fold. I must bring them also, and they will listen to my voice. So there will be one flock, one shepherd.* [17]*For this reason the Father loves me, because I lay down my life in order to take it up again.* [18]*No one takes it from me, but I lay it down of my own accord. I have power to lay it down, and I have power to take it up again. I have received this command from my Father."*

MATTHEW 11:25–30 [25]*At that time Jesus said, "I thank you, Father, Lord of heaven and earth, because you have hidden these things from the wise and the intelligent and have revealed them to infants;* [26]*yes, Father, for such was your gracious will.* [27]*All things have been handed over to me by my Father; and no one knows the Son except the Father, and no one knows the Father except the Son and anyone to whom the Son chooses to reveal him.*

[28]*"Come to me, all you that are weary and are carrying heavy burdens, and I will give you rest.* [29]*Take my yoke upon you, and learn from me; for I am gentle and humble in heart, and you will find rest for your souls.* [30]*For my yoke is easy, and my burden is light."*

The alto aria presents another aspect of the life of Jesus the Messiah. He is a gentle shepherd who cares for his flock and protects the young in his arms. The song is tender and pastoral, evoking the compassion of the good shepherd for his sheep. Through the intimate melody, we can imagine Jesus taking the lambs in his arms and holding them close to his heart.

These words of Isaiah are from the same section of the prophet that began *Messiah*. It is a continuation of the same hopeful tone evoked in "Comfort ye my people" and "O thou that tellest good tidings to Zion." Part 1 of *Messiah* is coming to a close in the same spirit of comfort and reassurance with which it began. God is coming to save his people and rescue them from their foes.

Sheep need a shepherd because they are virtually helpless to fend for themselves. The job of shepherding in Israel was not a task for a weakling. A shepherd's work involved long days and nights, exposed to harsh weather and the danger of wild animals. Sheep often wander off, fall into ravines, and become prey to robbers and wolves. The sheep are lost without the shepherd. Good shepherds must be vigilant, fearless, and willing to put their own lives at risk for the sake of the flock.

Israel's royal tradition often spoke of the shepherd-king. The king was responsible for caring for his people in the way that shepherds cared for their flocks. The shepherd-king must provide for his people, keep them safe from their enemies, and even fight for them against all who would wish to harm them. This image of the king was a reflection of God's care for the flock of Israel, a care that is both kind-hearted and fearless. Indeed, Isaiah presents this compassionate image after a reminder of God's awesome strength and power (Isa 40:10).

This self-sacrificing strength of the shepherd is presented in John's gospel in reference to Jesus, who "lays down his life for the sheep" (John 10:11). Unlike the hired hand, who runs away when he sees the wolf coming, the Messiah stands before his people as a strong but tender shepherd. He understands our faults and failings (John 10:14), but he has power over all the forces that threaten us.

The soprano aria "Come unto Him" follows the alto aria "He shall feed his flock," responding to Isaiah's words with the invitation of Matthew's gospel. The double arias are the same pastoral melody but in different keys. The soprano's entrance, taking over from the alto, is a beautiful musical moment. The melody of Isaiah's text about the tender care of the shepherd is elevated to a higher pitch and elaborated to express the words of the gospel text, inviting all people who are weary and burdened to come to him for rest.

Jesus spent a great deal of his earthly ministry bearing the burdens of others. He gave hope to the downtrodden, consoled the mournful, welcomed the outcasts, fed the hungry, and healed the sick. Matthew's text invites all who are burdened to come to Jesus, to experience his gentle yoke, to learn his ways, and to find rest in him. It is a wonderful response to all that we have been hearing about the ministry of the Messiah.

The oratorio of *Messiah* is not typical of Handel's other works in that there are no named characters and no dialogue. The usual drama between characters is absent, and the narration of *Messiah* is carried on by implication through the biblical texts. One of the ways in which the oratorio suppresses the drama is by taking words out of the mouth of Jesus and transforming them into third-person declarations. "Come unto me" and "Take my yoke upon you" becomes "Come unto Him" and "Take His yoke upon you." Jesus never speaks in *Messiah*, but the oratorio always points to him. By omitting any drama of personalities, the work becomes a reflection on the purpose of the Messiah's life in the world and an invitation to place our trust completely in him.

The chorus sings the final words of Part 1: "His yoke is easy, and His burthen is light." The chorus speaks for God's people, who have been liberated from the heavy and ill-fitting yoke of sin and guilt. The new yoke of God's grace frees us to live for God's kingdom. The music expresses this relief from the heavy yoke and the ease involved in obeying the way of Christ.

"Burthen," of course, is an archaic spelling of "burden." The easy yoke and light burden do not imply that the way of Jesus involves any lesser responsibilities than the law of Moses or any other religious system. After all, it was Jesus who said, "If any want to become my followers, let them deny themselves and take up their cross and follow me" (Matt 16:24). Our responsibilities become easy and light because our Messiah is "meek and lowly of heart." He would never load us with unnecessary burdens or ones beyond our ability to carry. He not only shows us the way to bear the yoke, but above all he carries it himself. The yoke placed on the disciples is first placed on Jesus. He invites us to come to him when we are weary and overloaded; he will bear our burdens and lighten our load.

Reflection and discussion

- In what way does the image of the shepherd confirm the tender compassion of the Messiah and also prepare for his passion and death?

- How can entrusting our burdens and cares to Jesus lighten our load?

- How can the way of discipleship, as described by Jesus (Matt 16:24), possibly be easy or restful?

Prayer

Gentle Shepherd, you feed your flock, carry the weak in your arms, and lead them to safety and rest. Feed me with the truth of your word, protect me from the dangers that threaten me, teach me to come to you in my weariness, and lead me in the way you have planned for my salvation.

SUGGESTIONS FOR FACILITATORS, GROUP SESSION 3

1. Welcome group members and ask if anyone has any announcements to make.

2. You may want to pray this prayer as a group:
Healing Savior, our lives are incomplete without the experience of your grace and forgiveness. Repair the wounds that sin has caused within us, heal our blindness to your truth, open our ears to the cry of your suffering people, and lift up our voices to give you praise. Fill the darkness with the light of your hope, banish the gloom of hatred and strife, and bring the justice of your reign upon the earth. Shepherd us in the way you have planned for our salvation, feed us with the truth of your word, protect us from the dangers that threaten us, and carry us in your arms to safety and rest.

3. Ask one or both of the following questions:
    - Which message of Scripture this week speaks most powerfully to you?
    - What is the most important lesson you learned through your study this week?

4. Discuss lessons 7 through 12. Choose one or more of the questions for reflection and discussion from each lesson to discuss as a group. You may want to ask group members which question was most challenging or helpful to them as you review each lesson.

5. Remember that there are no definitive answers for these discussion questions. The insights of group members will add to the understanding of all. None of these questions requires an expert.

6. After talking about each lesson, instruct group members to complete lessons 13 through 18 on their own during the six days before the next group meeting. They should write out their own answers to the questions as preparation for next week's group discussion.

7. Ask the group if anyone is having any particular problems with the Bible study during the week. You may want to share advice and encouragement within the group.

8. Conclude by praying aloud together the prayer at the end of one of the lessons discussed. You may add to the prayer based on the sharing that has occurred in the group.

LESSON 13  SESSION 4

John answered them, "I baptize with water. Among you stands one whom you do not know, the one who is coming after me; I am not worthy to untie the thong of his sandal." JOHN 1:26–27

Atonement through the Blood of the Lamb

22. CHORUS

Behold the Lamb of God that taketh away the sins of the world. (John 1:29)

JOHN 1:19–34 [19]*This is the testimony given by John when the Jews sent priests*
and Levites from Jerusalem to ask him, "Who are you?" [20]*He confessed and did not*
deny it, but confessed, "I am not the Messiah." [21]*And they asked him, "What then?*
Are you Elijah?" He said, "I am not." "Are you the prophet?" He answered, "No."
[22]*Then they said to him, "Who are you? Let us have an answer for those who sent*
us. What do you say about yourself?" [23]*He said,*

"I am the voice of one crying out in the wilderness,
'Make straight the way of the Lord,'"

as the prophet Isaiah said.

[24]*Now they had been sent from the Pharisees.* [25]*They asked him, "Why then are*
you baptizing if you are neither the Messiah, nor Elijah, nor the prophet?" [26]*John*
answered them, "I baptize with water. Among you stands one whom you do not
know, [27]*the one who is coming after me; I am not worthy to untie the thong of his*
sandal." [28]*This took place in Bethany across the Jordan where John was baptizing.*

[29]*The next day he saw Jesus coming toward him and declared, "Here is the*
Lamb of God who takes away the sin of the world! [30]*This is he of whom I said,*
'After me comes a man who ranks ahead of me because he was before me.' [31]*I*

myself did not know him; but I came baptizing with water for this reason, that he might be revealed to Israel." [32]*And John testified, "I saw the Spirit descending from heaven like a dove, and it remained on him.* [33]*I myself did not know him, but the one who sent me to baptize with water said to me, 'He on whom you see the Spirit descend and remain is the one who baptizes with the Holy Spirit.'* [34]*And I myself have seen and have testified that this is the Son of God."*

"Behold the Lamb of God" serves as an overture to Part 2 of *Messiah*, which will focus on the climax of the Messiah's redeeming work: his death and resurrection. The music is ominous and contrasts sharply with the exaltation of Part 1. The same chorus who sang the jubilant words "His yoke is easy and His burthen is light" now introduces Christ's passion. The liberation that made our yoke and burden light is contrasted with the heavy yoke of the Messiah's suffering which accomplished that liberation.

The coming of the Lamb of God is announced by John the Baptist at the beginning of Christ's ministry. The pronouncement encapsulates the meaning of the Gospel of John, the good news of redemption in the supreme sacrifice of Christ. John the Baptist pointed to Jesus in order to deflect the attention of the crowd away from himself and toward the true Redeemer. The Baptist called people to repentance, to turn away from sin, but only the Lamb of God "takes away the sin of the world."

In ancient Israel, the sacrificial rituals of the temple were understood to atone for the sins of God's people. The innocent lambs were the victims offered in sacrifice to God for individual and communal transgressions. "The sin of the world" is cosmic in its dimensions. It embraces all the violence, corruption, injustices, and evil at work throughout the world and throughout human history. The sacrifice of God's true Lamb offers divine forgiveness and atonement for all people everywhere.

The lamb of sacrifice was the most essential feature of Israel's great act of deliverance in the Exodus. The Passover defined the Israelites as a people and shaped their destiny. The sacrifice of the lamb provided nourishment for the journey from bondage, and the blood of the lamb marked the doorposts of the houses that would be saved from the death of the firstborn. John's gospel associates the sacrifice of Jesus with the Passover lamb by noting that the crucifixion of Jesus occurred at the very hour that the lambs were being sacrificed in Jerusalem's temple for the Passover feast. The sacrifice of the Lamb of God is the great act of the world's redemption. Through Israel's Messiah, the bonds of sin are broken and evil is vanquished forever.

The music of "Behold the Lamb" is shaped to express this divine undertaking. The melody line of "That taketh away the sin of the world" continually rises higher, depicting the heavy burden of sin being lifted from the world by the Redeemer's love unto death. Yet, this ascent isn't easy; it is slow and halting. Although his burden on us is light, our burden on him is heavy indeed. This music of the Lamb solemnly introduces the next several movements of the oratorio, which focus on the meaning of the Messiah's passion.

Reflection and discussion

- Why is "Lamb of God" an appropriate title of Jesus to introduce Part 2 of *Messiah*? What does this title tell me about the meaning of Christ's saving life and death?

- Why does John's gospel associate the crucifixion of Jesus with the sacrifice of the Passover lambs in the temple (19:14)? What is the meaning of Paul's exclamation "Our paschal lamb, Christ, has been sacrificed" (1 Cor 5:7)?

Prayer

Lamb of God, who takes away the sin of the world, have mercy on us. You took upon yourself the wooden yoke of the cross and bore the heavy burden of the world's sin. Help me to imitate your undying love and to unite my life with your redeeming sacrifice.

He was oppressed, and he was afflicted, yet he did not open his mouth; like a lamb that is led to the slaughter, and like a sheep that before its shearers is silent, so he did not open his mouth. ISAIAH 53:7

Our Wounded and Suffering Messiah

23. Aria (Alto)

He was despised and rejected of men; a man of sorrows and acquainted with grief. He gave His back to the smiters, and His cheeks to them that plucked off the hair. He hid not His face from shame and spitting. (Isaiah 53:3; 50:6)

24. CHORUS

Surely He hath borne our griefs, and carried our sorrows! He was wounded for our transgressions; He was bruised for our iniquities; the chastisement of our peace was upon Him. (Isaiah 53:4, 5)

25. CHORUS

And with His stripes we are healed. (Isaiah 53:5)

26. CHORUS

All we like sheep have gone astray; we have turned every one to his own way. And the Lord hath laid on Him the iniquity of us all. (Isaiah 53:6)

ISAIAH 53:1–9

1 *Who has believed what we have heard?*
And to whom has the arm of the Lord been revealed?
2 *For he grew up before him like a young plant,*
and like a root out of dry ground;
he had no form or majesty that we should look at him,
nothing in his appearance that we should desire him.
3 *He was despised and rejected by others;*
a man of suffering and acquainted with infirmity;
and as one from whom others hide their faces
he was despised, and we held him of no account.

4 *Surely he has borne our infirmities*
and carried our diseases;
yet we accounted him stricken,
struck down by God, and afflicted.
5 *But he was wounded for our transgressions,*
crushed for our iniquities;
upon him was the punishment that made us whole,
and by his bruises we are healed.
6 *All we like sheep have gone astray;*
we have all turned to our own way,
and the Lord has laid on him
the iniquity of us all.

7 *He was oppressed, and he was afflicted,*
yet he did not open his mouth;
like a lamb that is led to the slaughter,
and like a sheep that before its shearers is silent,
so he did not open his mouth.
8 *By a perversion of justice he was taken away.*
Who could have imagined his future?
For he was cut off from the land of the living,
stricken for the transgression of my people.

[9]They made his grave with the wicked
and his tomb with the rich,
although he had done no violence,
and there was no deceit in his mouth.

These four movements, the alto aria followed by three choruses, are taken from the Servant hymns of Isaiah. Originating in Israel's experience of exile, these hymns culminate in Isaiah 53, a meditation on the suffering of an innocent victim on behalf of others. The Israelite identity of this Servant is much debated. Some consider the Servant as a representative symbol for Israel, expressing the view that the sufferings of God's people in exile were redemptive for the nation. Others consider the Servant to be an individual figure, perhaps Jeremiah or Isaiah himself or a descendant of David. Christian tradition, probably even Jesus himself, identified the Servant with the Messiah.

The alto aria is a somber lament, inviting us to reflect on the Messiah's suffering. The low strings and frequent pauses between phrases increase the darkness and drama. The Servant's suffering was certainly a physical torment, but this passage emphasizes the psychological anguish as well. It is hard to imagine any type of suffering in human experience that Jesus did not experience. He was despised by his enemies and rejected by his friends. He was the innocent victim of betrayal, denial, abandonment, injustice, ridicule, and torture in one of the most painful deaths imaginable. Truly he was a "man of sorrows" (verse 3), drinking the cup of the pains and sadness of the human race to its bitter dregs.

The three choruses provide a contrast in rhythm and mood. This is the voice of God's people expressing the meaning of the Messiah's suffering. The emphatic "surely" accentuates the insight that his passion and death were for our sake. He has "borne our griefs and carried our sorrows"; he was "wounded for our transgressions" and "bruised for our iniquities" (verses 4–5). His sorrowful passion was not tragic fate, but an obedience that placed no limits on his self-giving love. "The chastisement of our peace," the punishment that restores us to wholeness, was placed upon God's Messiah. Since God's people had proven themselves incapable of turning from the tragedy of sin, and the sacrifice of animals had failed to atone for sin, God took a startling new course in accepting the self-offering of the gentle, compassionate, obedient Servant.

The central choral movement, "And with His stripes we are healed," expresses the profound mystery of redemptive love. The chorus lingers over the word "healed" as though a comforting balm were soothing the wound. Though he was innocent of any wrong, he took the consequences of our sin upon himself and poured himself out to death. In defiance of worldly wisdom and earthly power, he chose to make his life an instrument of God's healing. In an astonishing and mysterious way, the healing of humanity flows from the offering of the life of God's Messiah. The chorus is an expression of wonderment by a forgiven people.

The third chorus from Isaiah 53, expressing the waywardness of the sheep for whom the Lamb is slain, seems surprisingly lighthearted. The lost sheep meander aimlessly and hopelessly.

With clever tone painting, the phrase "gone astray" seems to fade away, and the phrase "we have turned" suggests the giddy and frenzied movement of the sheep. Sinners are like foolish sheep: wandering from the safety of the flock, falling into rushing streams, and thoughtlessly putting themselves in the path of predators. But with the final phrase, the confused activity ends, and the chorus confesses the seriousness of God's saving deed: "And the Lord hath laid on Him the iniquity of us all." The music moves in tortuously slow, descending notes as the voices enter, piling one atop the other in relentless layers of crushing weight while dramatically pausing on "Him." Finally, all the voices complete together the sentence "the iniquity of us all," expressing the burden of sin that the Messiah bore for us.

Reflection and discussion

- Based on the words of this hymn of the Suffering Servant, how would I explain the meaning and purpose of the Messiah's suffering and death?

- What benefits come to others because of the Servant's suffering? Why was he able to do what animal sacrifice in the temple had failed to do?

- What are examples of how the music expresses the various types of suffering experienced by the Messiah?

- In what ways does 1 Peter 2:21–25 apply the Suffering Servant hymn directly to the sacrifice of Jesus on the cross?

Prayer

Suffering Servant of God, you were despised, rejected, betrayed, abandoned, ridiculed, and tortured. Yet, you bore our grief and were wounded for our transgressions. Thank you for the sacrificial love through which you carried your cross and suffered. Open my heart to the healing and forgiveness that you offer me.

My God, my God, why have you forsaken me? Why are you so far from helping me, from the words of my groaning? O my God, I cry by day, but you do not answer; and by night, but find no rest. PSALM 22:1–2

The Messiah Mocked and Scorned

27. RECITATIVE (Tenor)

All they that see Him laugh Him to scorn; they shoot out their lips and shake their heads, saying: (Psalm 22:7)

28. CHORUS

He trusted in God that He would deliver Him; let Him deliver Him if He delight in Him. (Psalm 22:8)

PSALM 22:1–19

1 *My God, my God, why have you forsaken me?*
Why are you so far from helping me, from the words of my groaning?
2 *O my God, I cry by day, but you do not answer;*
and by night, but find no rest.

3 *Yet you are holy,*
enthroned on the praises of Israel.
4 *In you our ancestors trusted;*
they trusted, and you delivered them.

5 *To you they cried, and were saved;*
in you they trusted, and were not put to shame.

6 *But I am a worm, and not human;*
scorned by others, and despised by the people.
7 *All who see me mock at me;*
they make mouths at me, they shake their heads;
8 *"Commit your cause to the Lord; let him deliver—*
let him rescue the one in whom he delights!"

9 *Yet it was you who took me from the womb;*
you kept me safe on my mother's breast.
10 *On you I was cast from my birth,*
and since my mother bore me you have been my God.
11 *Do not be far from me,*
for trouble is near
and there is no one to help.

12 *Many bulls encircle me,*
strong bulls of Bashan surround me;
13 *they open wide their mouths at me,*
like a ravening and roaring lion.

14 *I am poured out like water,*
and all my bones are out of joint;
my heart is like wax;
it is melted within my breast;
15 *my mouth is dried up like a potsherd,*
and my tongue sticks to my jaws;
you lay me in the dust of death.

16 *For dogs are all around me;*
a company of evildoers encircles me.
My hands and feet have shriveled;
17 *I can count all my bones.*

They stare and gloat over me;
18 *they divide my clothes among themselves,*
and for my clothing they cast lots.

19 *But you, O Lord, do not be far away!*
O my help, come quickly to my aid!

The piercing recitative followed by the taunting chorus evokes the scene of Christ's crucifixion. Yet, rather than present us with the passion accounts of the gospels, the oratorio chooses the words of Psalm 22. The two verses chosen evoke the entire psalm of lament, the desperate cry of an Israelite in great distress.

The tenor recitative is sung to a frenzied accompaniment, and the hostile chorus suggests the mockery of the crowd. The words "deliver Him" are particularly harsh and scornful, and the word "delight" suggests jeering laughter. Here, the chorus is the taunting crowd expressing their bitter sarcasm at a public execution. But on another level, the chorus is the same people of God who sang the previous choral parts. The words express the unfaithfulness and distrust in all of us, the people for whom the Messiah gave his life.

The haunting Psalm 22 is a prayer of desperation. Its vocabulary is general enough to be prayed by readers of any time and place when faced with fear and threats. In such a frantic state, the psalmist feels totally alienated: from God ("why have you forsaken me?" verse 1), from other people ("there is no one to help," verse 11), and even from himself ("I am a worm, and not human," verse 6). Yet, the prayer is not one of utter despair; if God really has abandoned the psalmist, then why pray? The psalmist's desolation is brought on by the contradiction between what his ancestors had come to know—"they trusted, and you delivered them, to you they cried, and were saved" (verses 4–5)—and God's silence and seeming absence.

The gospel writers were influenced by Psalm 22 in writing their passion accounts. The words of the psalm echo the taunting of the crowds (verses 7–8), the division of Jesus' garments (verse 18), the thirst of Jesus on the cross (verse 15), and the torture of crucifixion (verses 14, 17). The opening verse, "My God, my God, why have you forsaken me?" is quoted by the dying Jesus in the gospels of Matthew and Mark.

The words of the psalm on the lips of Jesus and in the mouths of his scoffers are filled with irony. "He trusted in God," they jeer. They cannot see that even in his most distressing hour, he placed his trust in the God who would deliver him. Even when Jesus felt most forsaken by God, it was in this hour that God was most present to him. The psalm and the passion account teach us that if God can be present in the desperation of crucifixion, God cannot fail us in our own worst afflictions.

Reflection and discussion

- How does it feel to experience abandonment? In what ways did Jesus feel despised and rejected in his passion?

- How could the crowd who had welcomed Jesus into Jerusalem with jubilation so openly scorn him at the cross? In what sense does the crowd represent contradictory parts of my own life?

- How do I respond when feeling abandoned by God, family, and friends? Does it help to know that Jesus felt the same way?

Prayer

Suffering Savior, in the desperation of your crucifixion, you turned to God in distress. Teach me to trust that God will deliver me in the midst of the most difficult trials. May your cross always be the sign of my hope.

Draw near to me, redeem me, set me free because of my enemies.
You know the insults I receive, and my shame and dishonor;
my foes are all known to you. PSALM 69:18–19

The Brokenhearted Loneliness of the Cross

29. RECITATIVE (Tenor)

Thy rebuke hath broken His heart; He is full of heaviness. He looked for some to have pity on Him, but there was no man, neither found He any to comfort Him. (Psalm 69:20)

PSALM 69:9–20

9 *It is zeal for your house that has consumed me;*
the insults of those who insult you have fallen on me.
10 *When I humbled my soul with fasting,*
they insulted me for doing so.
11 *When I made sackcloth my clothing,*
I became a byword to them.
12 *I am the subject of gossip for those who sit in the gate,*
and the drunkards make songs about me.

13 *But as for me, my prayer is to you, O Lord.*
At an acceptable time, O God,
in the abundance of your steadfast love, answer me.
With your faithful help 14 *rescue me*

from sinking in the mire;
let me be delivered from my enemies
and from the deep waters.
15*Do not let the flood sweep over me,*
or the deep swallow me up,
or the Pit close its mouth over me.

16*Answer me, O Lord, for your steadfast love is good;*
according to your abundant mercy, turn to me.
17*Do not hide your face from your servant,*
for I am in distress—make haste to answer me.
18*Draw near to me, redeem me,*
set me free because of my enemies.

19*You know the insults I receive,*
and my shame and dishonor;
my foes are all known to you.
20*Insults have broken my heart,*
so that I am in despair.
I looked for pity, but there was none;
and for comforters, but I found none.

Psalm 69 is another hymn of lament, a song of desperation. We can imagine it being intoned in Jerusalem's temple as Jesus was dying on the cross outside the city walls. Like Psalm 22, it was sung by the early Christians as a passion psalm during Holy Week. The verse quoted in Handel's libretto is sung by the tenor in a mournful chant. Its complicated, meandering melody expresses the sufferer's torturous search for anyone who would show pity and his inability to find any comfort.

It is impossible to identify the psalmist or the cause of his suffering. "Sinking in the mire" and being swallowed up in the pit are metaphors for the power of death (verses 14–15). He is shamed and insulted without cause (verses 9–12, 19–20), and he prays for deliverance from distress (verses 16–18). Because the psalmist's suffering is described in general and metaphorical terms, the psalm can be prayed by all those in anguish and grief as an expression of their desperate condition and cry for help.

The distress of the psalmist is similar to that of the Suffering Servant of Isaiah 53. Both passages of Scripture were created in the historical period of Israel's exile. Out of the painful struggles of that period, a new understanding of suffering arose. The afflictions of God's people were understood not just as punishments for sin but also as part of the saving purpose of God for his people. Like the Suffering Servant, the psalmist is a man of sorrows who is despised and rejected by others. His suffering is not a result of punishment for his own sins; rather, he bears insult and injury out of devotion to God (verse 9).

Though the psalm did not originally refer to Israel's Messiah, it is understandable how the early Christians discerned in the psalm a way to understand the meaning of Jesus' passion. Psalm 69 is referred to more often in the New Testament than any other except Psalm 22, and the church has read it messianically since its earliest days (John 2:17; 15:25; Rom 15:3). Handel's libretto uses the psalm to emphasize the abandonment of Jesus at his cross and the loneliness of his death. The scene of Christ's passion was filled with alienation and hatred—the abandonment by his disciples, the indifference of the soldiers, the mockery of the crowd. Though *Messiah* opens with a promise of comfort to God's people (Isa 40:1), in the Messiah's darkest hour there was no one there to comfort him (Ps 69:20).

Reflection and discussion

- Why might Jesus have prayed this psalm during his passion? Which verse would I like to recall when I meditate on the cross?

- When have I felt the loneliest? How can the image of Jesus on the cross help me in times of loneliness?

- What is the effect on me when I pray Psalm 69 as if the "I" (subject) were Jesus? What difference does it make if I pray the psalm with myself as the subject?

- What does it mean to me that the central image of my faith is the battered corpse of a crucified man?

Prayer

Crucified Lord, on the cross you experienced loneliness and felt brokenhearted. When I look for sympathy and find insult, for comfort and find scorn, help me to look to your saving cross. Remain with me now and at the hour of my death.

For these things I weep; my eyes flow with tears; for a comforter is far from me, one to revive my courage; my children are desolate, for the enemy has prevailed. LAMENTATIONS 1:16

The Death of the Messiah

30. ARIA (Tenor)

Behold, and see if there be any sorrow like unto His sorrow. (Lamentations 1:12)

31. RECITATIVE (Tenor or Soprano)

He was cut off out of the land of the living; for the transgression of Thy people was He stricken. (Isaiah 53:8)

32. ARIA (Tenor or Soprano)

But Thou didst not leave His soul in hell; nor didst Thou suffer Thy Holy One to see corruption. (Psalm 16:10)

LAMENTATIONS 1:12–13, 16–17

12 Is it nothing to you, all you who pass by?
Look and see
if there is any sorrow like my sorrow,
which was brought upon me,
which the Lord inflicted
on the day of his fierce anger.

13 From on high he sent fire;
it went deep into my bones;

he spread a net for my feet;
he turned me back;
he has left me stunned,
faint all day long.

16 *For these things I weep;*
my eyes flow with tears;
for a comforter is far from me,
one to revive my courage;
my children are desolate,
for the enemy has prevailed.

17 *Zion stretches out her hands,*
but there is no one to comfort her;
the Lord has commanded against Jacob
that his neighbors should become his foes;
Jerusalem has become
a filthy thing among them.

PSALM 16:7–11

7 *I bless the Lord who gives me counsel;*
in the night also my heart instructs me.
8 *I keep the Lord always before me;*
because he is at my right hand, I shall not be moved.

9 *Therefore my heart is glad, and my soul rejoices;*
my body also rests secure.
10 *For you do not give me up to Sheol,*
or let your faithful one see the Pit.

11 *You show me the path of life.*
In your presence there is fullness of joy;
in your right hand are pleasures for evermore.

The tenor aria, "Behold and see if there be any sorrow," is mournful and melancholic. It is taken from the book of Lamentations, a series of dirges sung over the ruined city of Jerusalem after its fall to Babylonia in 587 BC. The book mourns the desolation of the city and the destruction of its walls, palaces, and especially its beloved temple. In the passage selected, the personified Jerusalem invites all who pass by to "look and see if there is any sorrow like my sorrow" (Lam 1:12). She weeps and reaches out her hands for reassurance, but "there is no one to comfort her" (Lam 1:17).

The libretto transforms the lamentation into a reflection on the terrible suffering that Christ endured. It bids us to look on his unparalleled sorrow while hanging on the cross. Though Jerusalem suffered for her own sins in the destruction of the temple by the Babylonians, and Christ suffered for the sins of others at the hands of the Romans, there is mutual anguish in the sorrow of Jerusalem and her Messiah. Like the city of his destiny, Jesus found no comfort from those he came to rescue from their transgressions.

The brief recitative returns to the Suffering Servant hymn to speak of the death and burial of God's Servant, though he had done no wrong (Isa 53:8–9). He was "stricken" not because of his own failures but because of the "transgression" of God's people. Out of his mercy and love, God sent his Servant to spare the people the consequences of their own sins. He stood with God's people in their guilt, and in God's mysterious plan he took their guilt upon himself. This costly act of redemption resulted in the sorrowful death of the Messiah: "He was cut off out of the land of the living."

From the mournful recitative, the stirring aria swells us, proclaiming that death is not the end of the story. Drawn from Psalm 16, the aria expresses the transitional movement from Christ's death on the cross to the triumph of Easter morning. God's Holy One had been placed in the grave, but he did not experience the bodily corruption of death.

Psalm 16 is a song of trust in God. The psalmist sings with confidence that God will not give him up to death but show him the path of life forever (Ps 16:10–11). Life for the Israelite is the joyful presence of God; the primary effect of death is the loss of God's presence. When the threat of death is removed, life is free for the complete joy of God's company, who alone can deliver from the darkness of death.

The word "hell" in the King James Version is an unfortunate translation. The Hebrew word is *sheol,* which means "grave" or "the realm of death." It does not refer to a place of punishment reserved for the wicked. Though the ancient Israelites had no clear conception of life after death, by the time of Jesus the doctrine of life after death was well established in Judaism. Early Christian theology developed the idea that after his death, Christ went to the underworld to proclaim the gospel to those who had already died (1 Pet 3:19; 4:6).

The Acts of the Apostles indicates that the apostolic church read Psalm 16 in the light of Christ's resurrection (Acts 2:24–32). Peter presented the psalm as expressing Christ's deliverance from death. The grave was powerless to claim God's Holy One "because it was impossible for him to be held in its power." The Messiah could not remain in the realm of death because he is the Lord of life.

Reflection and discussion

- Why would suffering and death be the means to attain the great victory of the Messiah? Do these texts offer me any insight into that mystery?

- How would I have responded to rumors of an empty tomb and sightings of the risen Christ? Does it seem too good to be true?

- How will my study of these texts from Messiah influence my sharing in the rituals of Holy Week?

Prayer

Holy One, your sorrow was more profound and your suffering more real than I can imagine. Your passion and death is the gateway to life everlasting and the fullness of joy. As I mediate on this unfathomable mystery, help me place my confidence in you.

They will receive blessing from the Lord, and vindication from the God of their salvation. Such is the company of those who seek him, who seek the face of the God of Jacob. PSALM 24:5–6

Death Cannot Restrain the King of Glory

33. CHORUS

Lift up your heads, O ye gates, and be ye lift up, ye everlasting doors, and the King of glory shall come in. Who is the King of glory? The Lord strong and mighty, the Lord mighty in battle. The Lord of hosts, He is the King of glory. (Psalm 24:7–10)

PSALM 24:1–10

1 *The earth is the Lord's and all that is in it,*
the world, and those who live in it;
2 *for he has founded it on the seas,*
and established it on the rivers.
3 *Who shall ascend the hill of the Lord?*
And who shall stand in his holy place?
4 *Those who have clean hands and pure hearts,*
who do not lift up their souls to what is false,
and do not swear deceitfully.
5 *They will receive blessing from the Lord,*
and vindication from the God of their salvation.
6 *Such is the company of those who seek him,*
who seek the face of the God of Jacob.

7*Lift up your heads, O gates!*
and be lifted up, O ancient doors!
that the King of glory may come in.
8*Who is the King of glory?*
The Lord, strong and mighty,
the Lord, mighty in battle.
9*Lift up your heads, O gates!*
and be lifted up, O ancient doors!
that the King of glory may come in.
10*Who is this King of glory?*
The Lord of hosts,
he is the King of glory.

Nowhere in the New Testament is the Messiah's transition from death to life described. There are reports of the empty tomb and witnesses who have seen the risen Lord truly and fully alive. But the event of resurrection itself is left as a mystery that cannot be portrayed. So, after mining the Hebrew Scriptures for the vocabulary of desolation, anguish, and sorrow to express the meaning of the cross, *Messiah* now searches the Scriptures for the language of triumph and glory to express the significance of Christ's resurrection.

With the proclamation of Christ's victory, the whole mood of *Messiah* changes. After expressing the dismal gloom of Christ's passion and death, the words and music explode into splendid praise. The somber tone of the passion gives way to the acclamation of resurrection. The joyous chorus, "Lift up your heads," expresses the triumphant return of the Messiah to his own people after his victory over the powers of death.

Psalm 24 was originally sung at a processional liturgy in which the ark of the covenant was brought back from a victorious battle and enthroned in its place of honor in Jerusalem's temple. The ark represented the mighty power of God on the battlefield and the royal presence of God ruling over the people from the temple of Zion. The Lord of hosts, an ancient title of Israel's God, is proclaimed as the King of glory, a divine title that appears nowhere else in the Bible. The gates of the city and temple are called to rise up to welcome the divine King and celebrate his sovereign reign.

Christian tradition offers this classic psalm a fuller meaning in light of the new covenant. The King of glory is the Messiah, victorious in his battle over sin and death, and reigning over the kingdom now inaugurated in the world. He reveals the true power and glory of God as never before. He is acclaimed as Savior of his people and Lord of the earth.

Like a coronation anthem, the music of *Messiah* soars in praise of the risen King. It is a celebration of divine victory. The one who was despised and battered in his passion is now proclaimed as the Lord of glory. Because of the dialogical nature of the psalm, with one group asking, "Who is the King of glory?" and another group answering the question, we are here presented with the oratorio's only antiphonal chorus. Following the sung dialogue, all the voices merge together in the grand and gripping chorus to affirm "The Lord of hosts, He is the King of Glory."

Reflection and discussion

- Which words and images indicate that Psalm 24 is a processional liturgy or entrance ritual? In what way could singing or reciting this psalm help me prepare for Sunday worship of God?

- In what way are the gates of my heart still closed to the King and his reign? How can I invite Christ into my life more fully?

Prayer

King of Glory, you have triumphed over the powers of sin and death. May I open the gates of my heart to you and invite you to assume your place as Lord of my life. Receive my praise and gratitude for your mighty works.

SUGGESTIONS FOR FACILITATORS, GROUP SESSION 4

1. Welcome group members and ask if anyone has any questions, announcements, or requests.

2. You may want to pray this prayer as a group:
   Suffering Savior, despised, rejected, betrayed, abandoned, ridiculed, and tortured, you took upon yourself the wooden yoke of the cross and bore the heavy burden of the world's sin. When we look for sympathy and find insults, for comfort and find scorn, help us look to your saving cross as the gateway to life everlasting and the fullness of joy. May we open the gates of our hearts to you, unite our lives with your redeeming sacrifice, place our confidence in you, and imitate your undying love.

3. Ask one or both of the following questions:
   - What is the most difficult part of this study for you?
   - What insights stand out to you from the lessons this week?

4. Discuss lessons 13 through 18. Choose one or more of the questions for reflection and discussion from each lesson to discuss as a group. You may want to ask group members which question was most challenging or helpful for them as you review each lesson.

5. Keep the discussion moving, but allow time for the questions that provoke the best discussion. Encourage the group members to use "I" language in their responses.

6. After talking over each lesson, instruct group members to complete lessons 19 through 24 on their own during the six days before the next group meeting. They should write out their own answers to the questions as preparation for next week's session.

7. Ask the group what encouragement they need for the coming week. Ask the members to pray for the needs of one another during the week.

8. Conclude by praying aloud together the prayer at the end of one of the lessons discussed. You may choose to conclude the prayer by asking members to pray aloud any requests they may have.

Of the angels he says, "He makes his angels winds, and his servants flames of fire." But of the Son he says, "Your throne, O God, is forever and ever, and the righteous scepter is the scepter of your kingdom." HEBREWS 1:7–8

God's Son Worshiped by All the Angels

34. RECITATIVE (Tenor)

Unto which of the angels said He at any time: Thou art my Son, this day have I begotten thee? (Hebrews 1:5)

35. CHORUS

Let all the angels of God worship Him. (Hebrews 1:6)

HEBREWS 1:1–9 [1]*Long ago God spoke to our ancestors in many and various ways by the prophets,* [2]*but in these last days he has spoken to us by a Son, whom he appointed heir of all things, through whom he also created the worlds.* [3]*He is the reflection of God's glory and the exact imprint of God's very being, and he sustains all things by his powerful word. When he had made purification for sins, he sat down at the right hand of the Majesty on high,* [4]*having become as much superior to angels as the name he has inherited is more excellent than theirs.*

[5]*For to which of the angels did God ever say,*
"You are my Son;
today I have begotten you"?
Or again,
"I will be his Father,
and he will be my Son"?

[6]And again, when he brings the firstborn into the world, he says,
"Let all God's angels worship him."
[7]Of the angels he says,
"He makes his angels winds,
and his servants flames of fire."
[8]But of the Son he says,
"Your throne, O God, is forever and ever,
and the righteous scepter is the scepter of your kingdom.
[9]You have loved righteousness and hated wickedness;
therefore God, your God, has anointed you
with the oil of gladness beyond your companions."

Handel's *Messiah* does not narrate the events associated with the resurrection—the discovery of the empty tomb, the appearance in the Upper Room, the encounter at Emmaus, or the lakeside appearance—just as it does not narrate the birth, life, or crucifixion of Jesus. Instead we are invited to reflect on the meaning and consequences of the resurrection. In quoting the book of Hebrews, the oratorio brings us into the heavenly courts to celebrate with the angels the achievement of the Messiah's mission.

The book of Hebrews presents Jesus Christ as the great High Priest of the heavenly temple. Having offered himself as the singular sacrifice for the world, he continually intercedes for humanity in the Father's presence. The sanctuary of the earthly Jerusalem and its daily offerings are described as mere shadows of the heavenly temple and the eternal sacrifice of Christ. As the book begins, the author proclaims that Jesus is God's Son, the "heir of all things," worthy to receive the worship of the entire heavenly court. "When he had made purification for sins," he took his rightful place in heaven, higher in honor than even the angels (verses 1–4).

The tenor recitative asks a rhetorical question: "Unto which of the angels said He at any time: Thou art my Son, this day have I begotten thee?" (verse 5). Of course, the answer is that none of the angels were ever begotten of God and declared God's Son. The angels are "servants" of God (verse 7), whereas the Son has inherited the divine throne and rules over God's kingdom (verse 8). On earth Jesus took on the role of the servant, yet in his divine nature he retained the identity and honor of the Son of God. With his resurrection, his dignity as Son was recognized and proclaimed.

The quotation "Thou art my Son, this day have I begotten thee" is taken from Psalm 2, a royal psalm composed for the anointing and enthronement of Israel's kings. The psalm refers to God's promise to King David concerning the royal heir: "I will be a father to him, and he shall be a son to me" (2 Sam 7:14). The early Christians recognized this psalm as fulfilled in the Messiah, the Son of God not merely by human adoption but in his divine being: "Begotten, not made, consubstantial with the Father." Having won the cosmic battle over sin and death, the Son takes his throne, superior to all the angels of the heavenly court.

The chorus is exultant: "Let all the angels of God worship Him." Like an earthly shadow of the heavenly choirs, Handel's chorus beckons us to join in the praise. God's purposes in sending his Son into the world have been accomplished, and now we on earth can stand united with heaven to worship the Messiah.

Reflection and discussion

- In what ways does Hebrews 1:1–9 confirm the divine nature of Jesus Christ? What difference does it make to me that he is "the reflection of God's glory and the exact imprint of God's very being" (verse 3)?

- In what way is the throne of Israel's king a shadow of the heavenly throne of God's Son? How does the royal rule of the earthly king prefigure the eternal reign of the Messiah?

Prayer

Son of God, you are higher in honor than all the angels of God and receive the worship of God's heavenly court. I praise you with all the heavenly choirs, for you have conquered death by your eternal sacrifice.

You ascended the high mount, leading captives in your train and receiving gifts from people, even from those who rebel against the Lord God's abiding there. Blessed be the Lord, who daily bears us up; God is our salvation. PSALM 68:18–19

The Ascended Lord Offers Gifts to His People

36. ARIA (Bass, Alto, or Soprano)

Thou art gone up on high; Thou hast led captivity captive, and received gifts for men, yea, even for Thine enemies, that the Lord God might dwell among them. (Psalm 68:18)

37. CHORUS

The Lord gave the word; great was the company of the preachers. (Psalm 68:11)

PSALM 68:1–20

1 Let God rise up, let his enemies be scattered;
let those who hate him flee before him.
2 As smoke is driven away, so drive them away;
as wax melts before the fire,
let the wicked perish before God.
3 But let the righteous be joyful;
let them exult before God;
let them be jubilant with joy.

4 *Sing to God, sing praises to his name;*
lift up a song to him who rides upon the clouds—
his name is the Lord—
be exultant before him.

5 *Father of orphans and protector of widows*
is God in his holy habitation.
6 *God gives the desolate a home to live in;*
he leads out the prisoners to prosperity,
but the rebellious live in a parched land.

7 *O God, when you went out before your people,*
when you marched through the wilderness,
8 *the earth quaked, the heavens poured down rain*
at the presence of God, the God of Sinai,
at the presence of God, the God of Israel.
9 *Rain in abundance, O God, you showered abroad;*
you restored your heritage when it languished;
10 *your flock found a dwelling in it;*
in your goodness, O God, you provided for the needy.

11 *The Lord gives the command;*
great is the company of those who bore the tidings:
12 *"The kings of the armies, they flee, they flee!"*
The women at home divide the spoil,
13 *though they stay among the sheepfolds—*
the wings of a dove covered with silver,
its pinions with green gold.
14 *When the Almighty scattered kings there,*
snow fell on Zalmon.

15 *O mighty mountain, mountain of Bashan;*
O many-peaked mountain, mountain of Bashan!
16 *Why do you look with envy, O many-peaked mountain,*

at the mount that God desired for his abode,
where the Lord will reside forever?

17*With mighty chariotry, twice ten thousand,*
thousands upon thousands,
the Lord came from Sinai into the holy place.
18*You ascended the high mount,*
leading captives in your train
and receiving gifts from people,
even from those who rebel against the Lord God's abiding there.
19*Blessed be the Lord,*
who daily bears us up;
God is our salvation.
20*Our God is a God of salvation,*
and to God, the Lord, belongs escape from death.

EPHESIANS 4:7–13 7*But each of us was given grace according to the measure of*
Christ's gift. 8*Therefore it is said,*
"When he ascended on high he made captivity itself a captive;
he gave gifts to his people."
9*(When it says, "He ascended," what does it mean but that he had also descended*
into the lower parts of the earth? 10*He who descended is the same one who ascended*
far above all the heavens, so that he might fill all things.) 11*The gifts he gave were*
that some would be apostles, some prophets, some evangelists, some pastors and
teachers, 12*to equip the saints for the work of ministry, for building up the body of*
Christ, 13*until all of us come to the unity of the faith and of the knowledge of the*
Son of God, to maturity, to the measure of the full stature of Christ.

The jubilant aria "Thou art gone up on high" completes the scene of Christ's triumph. His victory is sung with verses from Psalm 68, originally a psalm celebrating God's ascent to his temple after a victorious battle. The early Christians chose these verses as a reference to Christ's ascension and his bestowal of gifts of the Spirit upon his church.

The New Testament letter to the Ephesians quotes Psalm 68:18, "When he ascended on high he made captivity itself a captive; he gave gifts to his people" (Eph 4:8). Paul sees the psalm's prophetic fulfillment in the ascension of Christ. Having made "captive" every power that holds humanity in captivity, namely the powers of evil, sin, and death, Christ could now bestow divine gifts upon all his people. While the ascended Christ was no longer bodily present on earth, he could now distribute those gifts that would enable his church to carry his victory into the whole world. Paul teaches that those gifts are the various types of ministry—apostles, prophets, evangelists, pastors, and teachers. All of these are gifts of the Spirit which involve preaching and proclaiming the good news of Jesus Christ.

The bold and confident chorus, "The Lord gave the word; great was the company of the preachers," expresses the command to begin the evangelizing work of the church. Again, the libretto uses the victory song of Psalm 68 to express the missionary command of Christ. Originally, the psalm referred to God's command to proclaim the good tidings of Israel's victory in battle as the enemy kings and their armies flee (Ps 68:11–12). In Handel's work, "the company of the preachers" are the heralds of the Messiah, those sent out to proclaim the good tidings of Christ's death and resurrection.

The writings of Luke—his gospel and the Acts of the Apostles—recount the ascension of Jesus and the descent of the Holy Spirit (Luke 24:51; Acts 1:8–11; Acts 2). Again, *Messiah* does not narrate these events but proclaims their significance and their results for God's people. Jesus returned to the Father and sent the Spirit upon the church so that the worldwide mission could begin. Jesus had won the victory of life, but it would take a great company of preachers to bring the good tidings of his salvation to the whole world. The Acts of the Apostles tells the story of that work: moving from Jerusalem throughout the ancient world, through hardship and persecution, by land and by sea to the ends of the earth.

Reflection and discussion

- Why is the ascension of Christ the moment that he may extend gifts upon his church? What spiritual gifts is he bestowing upon me?

- With the departure of Jesus, the mission of spreading the gospel falls to us. In what way am I a "preacher" of the good news of Christ to others?

- In what ways does the chorus express the saving power of God's word when it is preached to the world?

Prayer

Triumphant Lord, by your death and resurrection you conquered the cosmic forces that enslaved humanity. Liberated by your victory, help me to be a witness to life's goodness and purpose for those I meet each day.

The Lord has bared his holy arm before the eyes of all the nations; and all the ends of the earth shall see the salvation of our God.

ISAIAH 52:10

Announcing the Reign of Our God

38. ARIA (Alto and Soprano)

How beautiful are the feet of him that bringeth good tidings of salvation; that saith unto Zion, Thy God reigneth! (Isaiah 52:7)

CHORUS

Break forth into joy. (Isaiah 52:9)

ISAIAH 52:7–10

[7]*How beautiful upon the mountains*
are the feet of the messenger who announces peace,
who brings good news,
who announces salvation,
who says to Zion, "Your God reigns."
[8]*Listen! Your sentinels lift up their voices,*
together they sing for joy;
for in plain sight they see
the return of the Lord to Zion.
[9]*Break forth together into singing,*
you ruins of Jerusalem;

for the Lord has comforted his people,
he has redeemed Jerusalem.
10*The Lord has bared his holy arm*
before the eyes of all the nations;
and all the ends of the earth shall see
the salvation of our God.

This exquisite aria is an expressive meditation on the long-awaited message of the gospel. The messenger bears wonderful news for all the people—the glad tidings of salvation. The "feet" of the messenger are "beautiful" because they carry the message that people have longed to hear. He announces the most magnificent proclamation for all God's people: "Your God reigns."

The high-spirited chorus then urges the listeners to join in the exuberant celebration: "Break forth into joy." For a long time it had looked like God was not winning the battle over God's enemies. The forces of evil, sin, and death had captured God's people and held them imprisoned. But now the period of exile is ended because the Messiah has conquered the powers that kept God's people captive, and he has established the reign of God.

Once again, we return to that section of Isaiah's preaching in which the prophet offered comforting and hopeful words to the people of Jerusalem taken into exile by the Babylonians. Here he describes a prophetic vision of a military courier, running to Jerusalem to convey the news of God's victory. This triumph over Babylon will set God's people free and restore Jerusalem to its former glory.

As the runner is about to complete his long journey across the desert from Babylon, he appears over the crest of the mountains that surround Jerusalem. His feet are bruised and torn after the long run, yet of those feet the prophet exclaims, "How beautiful!" for these are the feet that bring words that thrill the heart. At the end of his journey, the messenger proclaims the good news of peace and salvation, and then he declares the climactic and breathless decree: "Your God reigns" (verse 7).

The sentinels standing watch over the city are the first to see the approaching runner and to hear his message. They take up the joyful cry because they understand at once that the return of the people from Babylon is "the return of the Lord to Zion" (verse 8). Even the ruins of Jerusalem are summoned to join in the drama of restoration by singing for joy. The opening words of the prophet of the exile, "Comfort, O comfort my people" (Isa 40:1), are being fulfilled: "The Lord has comforted his people, he has redeemed Jerusalem" (verse 9).

God's return to Jerusalem is described as an event of global proportions. "All the nations" witness God's victory, a salvation that affects "all the ends of the earth" (verse 10). God's restoration of his people is an event that gives hope to all people in bondage. It gives orientation to those who feel lost and renewal to those who experience the crushing sadness of grief. For all defeated and disillusioned people everywhere, the messenger's cry is the hopeful and final word: "Your God reigns."

Handel's *Messiah,* like early Christian writers, applies these prophetic words of Isaiah to the early Christian missionaries. After the resurrection of Jesus and the empowerment by his Spirit, these evangelists of the church brought the gospel to all the ends of the earth. We honor the beautiful feet of Peter, Paul, Barnabas, Phoebe, Priscilla, Aquila, and countless others through the centuries who have proclaimed the good tidings of salvation throughout the world.

Reflection and discussion

- How do this aria and chorus express the beauty and joy of the gospel, "the good tidings of salvation"?

- What can I learn from this passage of Isaiah about the church's call to evangelize and proclaim the message of the gospel to others?

- In what ways is the proclamation of Jerusalem's liberation from Babylon fulfilled or completed in the announcement of the gospel?

- In what way are my "feet" engaged in the service of God's reign? How can I better use my feet for the work of the gospel?

Prayer

Messiah and Lord, you reign over my life and over the whole world. I praise you with joy for the opportunity of serving you. Inspire me to be your messenger, bringing your good news of peace and salvation to the world in which I live.

So faith comes from what is heard, and what is heard comes through the word of Christ. But I ask, have they not heard? Indeed they have; for "Their voice has gone out to all the earth, and their words to the ends of the world." ROMANS 10:17–18

Bringing the Good News to All the World

39. CHORUS

Their sound is gone out into all lands, and their words unto the ends of the world. (Psalm 19:4; Romans 10:18)

PSALM 19:1–4

1 *The heavens are telling the glory of God;*
and the firmament proclaims his handiwork.
2 *Day to day pours forth speech,*
and night to night declares knowledge.
3 *There is no speech, nor are there words;*
their voice is not heard;
4 *yet their voice goes out through all the earth,*
and their words to the end of the world.

ROMANS 10:11–18 11 *The scripture says, "No one who believes in him will be put to shame."*

[12]For there is no distinction between Jew and Greek; the same Lord is Lord of
all and is generous to all who call on him. [13]For, "Everyone who calls on the name
of the Lord shall be saved."
[14]But how are they to call on one in whom they have not believed? And how are
they to believe in one of whom they have never heard? And how are they to hear
without someone to proclaim him? [15]And how are they to proclaim him unless
they are sent? As it is written, "How beautiful are the feet of those who bring good
news!" [16]But not all have obeyed the good news; for Isaiah says, "Lord, who has
believed our message?" [17]So faith comes from what is heard, and what is heard
comes through the word of Christ.
[18]But I ask, have they not heard? Indeed they have; for
"Their voice has gone out to all the earth,
and their words to the ends of the world."

This aggressive and confident chorus expresses the worldwide scope of the disciples' evangelizing mission. Soprano, alto, tenor, and bass, one after the other, sing the theme: "Their song has gone out." Then the chorus sings the destination of the messengers: "into all lands…unto the ends of the world." The music is expansive, as is the universal range of the mission.

At the end of his earthly work, Jesus commissioned his disciples to continue his work and bring the gospel to the whole world: "Go therefore and make disciples of all nations" (Matt 28:19). At his ascension, Jesus told the disciples not to continue looking toward heaven because they had work to do on the earth: "You will be my witnesses in Jerusalem, in all Judea and Samaria, and to the ends of the earth" (Acts 1:8). The saving work of Jesus is not a private spirituality; it is the gospel destined to be announced and disseminated to the whole world.

Messiah again uses an ancient psalm to proclaim the universal destiny of the gospel. Psalm 19 describes how the vastness of creation proclaims the glory of God. The heavens, in their beauty and expanse, give witness and praise to their creator (Ps 19:1). In universal choral antiphony, the daylight declares God's glory while the firmament of night sings God's praises (Ps 19:2). Unlike a human congregation, they cannot sing with speech and language, yet their "voice" and their "words" go out to the ends of the world in witness to God (Ps 19:3–4). The universe sings a never-ending concert in praise of its creator. Paul speaks of this natural revelation in his letter to the Romans: "Ever since the creation of the world his eternal power and divine nature, invisible though they are, have been understood and seen through the things he has made" (Rom 1:20).

In another section of his letter, Paul speaks about the universality of God's call to salvation in Christ, without distinction between Jew and Greek. Salvation is offered without limits; it is a universal promise for everyone who calls on the Lord and believes (Rom 10:12–13). Yet, the gospel must always be incarnated; God's saving word must be communicated through human beings. It is impossible to come to belief unless one has first heard the saving message from those entrusted with its proclamation (Rom 10:14–15).

Paul took seriously his divine commission to make disciples of all the nations and to witness Christ to the ends of the earth. He calls upon all believers in Christ to bring the good news to others. Since faith is awakened by hearing the message of salvation, Christians must be bearers of the gospel to all the earth (Rom 10:17–18).

Reflection and discussion

- According to Psalm 19, how does creation give witness to God's goodness? In what way does Paul agree with the psalmist?

- Why is human communication so necessary for the spread of the gospel to the world? Why do I often hesitate to use words to express the message of salvation to others?

- In what ways do the chorus and orchestra musically illustrate the call to bring the good news to all the corners of the world?

- Why must the word of God be incarnated in human lives in order to be proclaimed, heard, and believed (Rom 10:14–15)?

- How does Paul's teaching in Romans 10 emphasize the importance of evangelization? What is my responsibility in this mission of the church?

Prayer

Lord of all peoples, you commanded your disciples to be your witnesses to the ends of the earth. Show me how to make disciples by participating in the evangelizing mission of your church. May my life be a demonstration of the good news and the joy of your salvation.

I will tell of the decree of the Lord: He said to me, "You are my son; today I have begotten you. Ask of me, and I will make the nations your heritage, and the ends of the earth your possession.

PSALM 2:7–8

God's Messiah Challenges Earthly Powers

40. ARIA (Bass)

Why do the nations so furiously rage together, why do the people imagine a vain thing? The kings of the earth rise up, and the rulers take counsel together against the Lord, and His anointed. (Psalm 2:1, 2)

41. CHORUS

Let us break their bonds asunder, and cast away their yokes from us. (Psalm 2:3)

42. RECITATIVE (Tenor)

He that dwelleth in Heaven shall laugh them to scorn; the Lord shall have them in derision. (Psalm 2:4)

43. ARIA (Tenor)

Thou shalt break them with a rod of iron; Thou shall dash them in pieces like a potter's vessel. (Psalm 2:9)

PSALM 2:1–12

1*Why do the nations conspire,*
and the peoples plot in vain?
2*The kings of the earth set themselves,*
and the rulers take counsel together,
against the Lord and his anointed, saying,
3*"Let us burst their bonds asunder,*
and cast their cords from us."

4*He who sits in the heavens laughs;*
the Lord has them in derision.
5*Then he will speak to them in his wrath,*
and terrify them in his fury, saying,
6*"I have set my king on Zion, my holy hill."*

7*I will tell of the decree of the Lord:*
He said to me, "You are my son;
today I have begotten you.
8*Ask of me, and I will make the nations your heritage,*
and the ends of the earth your possession.
9*You shall break them with a rod of iron,*
and dash them in pieces like a potter's vessel."

10*Now therefore, O kings, be wise;*
be warned, O rulers of the earth.
11*Serve the Lord with fear,*
with trembling 12*kiss his feet,*
or he will be angry, and you will perish in the way;
for his wrath is quickly kindled.

Happy are all who take refuge in him.

Though the Messiah has conquered the powers of the world and the word of salvation has been proclaimed, the message is rejected by many and the Messiah's reign is resisted by the kingdoms of the earth. Here the bass, chorus, and tenor sing selections from Psalm 2, one of the great enthronement hymns of Israel's monarchy. The text proclaims hope and confidence in the Messiah's triumph despite the persistence of human rebellion.

This ancient royal psalm asserts that the installation of Israel's king on the holy mount is an act of God (verse 6). It expresses astonishment that the kingdoms of the earth and their rulers would rebel against the dominion of "the Lord and his anointed" (verses 1–2). God's anointed one (*messiah*, in Hebrew) is designated as God's son, begotten by God on the day of his enthronement, and he is given the right and power to rule the world (verses 7–8). The rulers of the earth are urged to stop defying God's rule and to take refuge in him (verses 10–11).

Though this psalm was composed for the enthronement of the royal successors of King David, Israel's history indicates that its language is idealistic. Israel was always a minor state, sandwiched between the rule of Egypt to the West and Assyria or Babylon to the East. None of these kingdoms of the earth ever trembled in fear at the rule of the kingdom of David in Jerusalem. Only when there was a power vacuum between these earthly empires could Israel even hope for independence. Yet, even after the historical monarchy had completely collapsed, God's people preserved this psalm as an expression of their hope. They knew that the psalm proclaims something greater than the historical influence of Jerusalem's royal court. God had promised to send his Messiah, the anointed one in the line of David, to restore the kingdom.

Psalm 2 became the most important psalm for the early Christians as they sought to express the significance of Christ in terms of the ancient Hebrew Scriptures. This psalm is the only place in the Old Testament that speaks of God's king, God's messiah, and God's son in the same text. These royal designations in ancient Israel became important titles of Jesus in the New Testament, and it is in this Christian context that Handel's *Messiah* uses these verses of Psalm 2 to express the victorious enthronement of Christ and his rule over all humanity.

The bass aria interprets the opening words of the psalm. The vocal line paints in sound the struggle between the rulers of the earth and the reign of

God, while the tremolo of the string accompaniment expresses the frenzy and fury of the nations as they rage against the Messiah. The religious authorities and Roman rulers of Jerusalem had conspired against him, with the imperial powers of Rome pronouncing the death sentence and its soldiers carrying it out. While Jesus died on the cross, it looked as though the earthly powers had prevailed over the forces of goodness, truth, and love. But the resurrection dramatically reversed that conclusion as God gave the power to rule the world to his Messiah. In the Acts of the Apostles, Peter and John quote these verses of the psalm as they recall how "both Herod and Pontius Pilate" gathered together against Jesus, and the apostles pray for the courage to preach the gospel despite hostility and persecution (Acts 4:24–31).

The taunting chorus, "Let us break their bonds asunder, and cast away their yokes from us," expresses the rebellious plot of the insurgents against God and his Messiah. The contrapuntal voices represent the various powers that revolt in opposition to God's rule, while the melisma on the word "away" depicts the struggling forces attempting to rid themselves of divine sovereignty.

The tenor recitative and aria express the absurdity of the notion that any worldly powers can defeat the forces of goodness and love manifested in Christ's teaching, healing, death, and resurrection. The violent, military idiom of the psalm is transformed into an evangelical mode through the life of Jesus, but the power expressed in the images remains. God "laughs" at the impossible attempts of rebellious rulers to overturn Christ's victory and knows that their plans will be smashed as easily as an iron rod shatters a clay vessel. God's reign is established by the one who ultimately controls the destiny of all nations and powers.

Reflection and discussion

- What comfort does the psalm provide in the face of rebellion by the worldly powers?

- In what ways does the music express the rage and frenzy of those who reject the good news of salvation?

- In what ways is the message and reign of the Messiah resisted and rejected today?

- Why do I believe that the divine powers of love, truth, and goodness will conquer the opposing forces in the world? What gives me hope for the future of God's reign?

Prayer

Anointed One of God, you were rejected by many during your ministry on earth, and many continue to resist your reign. Give me hope in your ultimate victory, especially when its evidence is so difficult to see in the world. Make me an instrument of your reign on earth.

His eyes are like a flame of fire, and on his head are many diadems; and he has a name inscribed that no one knows but himself. He is clothed in a robe dipped in blood, and his name is called The Word of God. REVELATION 19:12–13

King of Kings and Lord of Lords

44. CHORUS

Hallelujah! For the Lord God Omnipotent reigneth. The kingdom of this world is become the kingdom of our Lord, and of His Christ; and He shall reign for ever and ever. King of Kings, and Lord of Lords. Hallelujah! (Revelation 19:6; 11:15; 19:16)

REVELATION 11:15–19 [15]*Then the seventh angel blew his trumpet, and there were loud voices in heaven, saying,*

"The kingdom of the world has become the kingdom of our Lord
and of his Messiah,
and he will reign forever and ever."

[16]*Then the twenty-four elders who sit on their thrones before God fell on their faces and worshiped God,* [17]*singing,*

"We give you thanks, Lord God Almighty,
who are and who were,
for you have taken your great power
and begun to reign.
[18]*The nations raged,*

but your wrath has come,
and the time for judging the dead,
for rewarding your servants, the prophets
and saints and all who fear your name,
both small and great,
and for destroying those who destroy the earth."

[19]Then God's temple in heaven was opened, and the ark of his covenant was seen within his temple; and there were flashes of lightning, rumblings, peals of thunder, an earthquake, and heavy hail.

REVELATION 19:6–16 *[6]Then I heard what seemed to be the voice of a great multitude, like the sound of many waters and like the sound of mighty thunder-peals, crying out,*

"Hallelujah!
For the Lord our God
the Almighty reigns.
[7]Let us rejoice and exult
and give him the glory,
for the marriage of the Lamb has come,
and his bride has made herself ready;
[8]to her it has been granted to be clothed
with fine linen, bright and pure"—

for the fine linen is the righteous deeds of the saints.

[9]And the angel said to me, "Write this: Blessed are those who are invited to the marriage supper of the Lamb." And he said to me, "These are true words of God."
[10]Then I fell down at his feet to worship him, but he said to me, "You must not do that! I am a fellow servant with you and your comrades who hold the testimony of Jesus. Worship God! For the testimony of Jesus is the spirit of prophecy."

[11]Then I saw heaven opened, and there was a white horse! Its rider is called
Faithful and True, and in righteousness he judges and makes war. [12]His eyes are like
a flame of fire, and on his head are many diadems; and he has a name inscribed that
no one knows but himself. [13]He is clothed in a robe dipped in blood, and his name is
called The Word of God. [14]And the armies of heaven, wearing fine linen, white and
pure, were following him on white horses. [15]From his mouth comes a sharp sword

with which to strike down the nations, and he will rule them with a rod of iron; he will tread the wine press of the fury of the wrath of God the Almighty. [16]*On his robe and on his thigh he has a name inscribed, "King of kings and Lord of lords."*

The Hallelujah chorus is widely regarded as the climax of Handel's *Messiah.* It is one of the most magnificent pieces of music ever written. A popular legend claims that King George II was so moved by the music at its premier performance in London that he rose to his feet when he heard it, requiring that his subjects do the same. Though there is some doubt over the historical accuracy of this story, the popular custom of standing during the chorus is followed in performances throughout the world.

Handel included trumpets and timpani in this chorus to emphasize its triumphal character. Throughout the Bible, rumbling thunder manifests God's presence, and trumpets are sounded to summon Israel to battle, to call God's people to repentance, to install new kings, and to convene worshippers for solemn feasts. In the book of Revelation, the angels blow trumpets to express alarm and terror, but the final trumpet sounds the climax of God's triumph over evil and the announcement of his reign (11:15). It is accompanied by an outburst of rejoicing in heaven and calls God's people to a victory celebration: "The kingdom of the world has become the kingdom of our Lord and of his Messiah."

Of course, the whole earth has always belonged to God by creation, but this world and its people rebelled against God's rule. Although God's grace and love were still active, the world lost its purpose and rejected God's reign over it. But with the victory of Christ's cross and resurrection, the destiny of humanity and all creation has changed direction. The kingdom of the world has been redeemed and all earthly powers and rulers are under the authority of the Lord and his Messiah.

As all of heaven gives thanks, God's temple in heaven opens and the ark of the covenant—the sacramental sign of God's presence which only the high priest was allowed to see—may be seen by all God's people (11:19). The gospels tell us that at the death of Jesus, the veil of the temple was torn in two (Mark 15:38). This was the veil that separated the holy of holies, where the ark of the covenant once stood, from God's people. Both the gospels and Revelation express the same reality: access to the presence of God is now offered to all people. The heavenly scene expresses the eternal results of Christ's saving actions on earth. With the earthly victory of God's Messiah, the world is redeemed, the kingdom belongs to God, sin and death are defeated forever, and God's saving presence is open to all.

The book of Revelation offered hope to the early Christians as they sought to be committed to Christ in the midst of a hostile culture. Those Christians were a tiny but growing minority, but they were scattered throughout the entire Roman empire among many ethnic groups. The vicious persecutions challenged their fidelity and many chose to witness their faith to the point of suffering death. The apocalyptic writing of Revelation expresses the struggle between the way of Christ and the evils of the empire through the contrasting images of the Lamb and the beasts. Those who remain faithful are the bride of Christ, those called to the marriage banquet of the Lamb (19:7–9).

The victorious Christ is also presented as a hero riding a white horse. Yet, this champion does not conquer with violence or vengeance. His cloak is dipped in his own blood as he charges out to conquer with the power of his self-sacrificing love (19:13). His only weapon comes from his mouth, the sharp sword of the gospel proclaimed (19:15). His identifying title is "King of kings and Lord of lords" (19:16).

This is the victorious Messiah. At his conquest, we all sing "Hallelujah," a Hebrew word which means "Praise the Lord." This is no temporary revolution, but a decisive triumph over the beastly powers of evil and death. We join in his victory, not through hatred and hostility, but through faithful witness, patient resistance, generous suffering, and confident trust. If we follow him, we shall reign with him forever and ever.

Reflection and discussion

- What is the reason why the chorus offers triumphant praise to the Lord?

- Why is the victory of Christ symbolized by a great battle? What parts of the imagery convince me that Christ did not triumph through aggression and violence?

- Why does Revelation depict the holy of holies and the ark of the covenant in the heavenly vision? In what way does this vision express the consequences of Christ's death on the cross?

- In what way does confidence in the triumph of Christ spur me to work for justice in the world? What are my frustrations and my hopes?

Prayer

King of kings and Lord of lords, you are victorious over all the forces I fear. Help me to experience your victory in my own heart and to be faithful and true to your word. Strengthen your church as we wait for your return in glory.

SUGGESTIONS FOR FACILITATORS, GROUP SESSION 5

1. Welcome group members and ask if anyone has any questions, announcements, or requests.

2. You may want to pray this prayer as a group:
   Triumphant Lord, who by your death and resurrection have conquered the cosmic forces that enslaved humanity, may we experience your liberating victory and be faithful to your word. Make us instruments of your reign on earth and give us hope in your ultimate victory. As you commanded your disciples to be your witness to the ends of the earth, show us how to make disciples by participating in the evangelizing mission of your church. May our lives demonstrate the good news and the joy of your salvation.

3. Ask one or both of the following questions:
   - What most intrigued you from this week's study?
   - How do the questions of Jesus help me to ask better questions of others?

4. Discuss lessons 19 through 24. Choose one or more of the questions for reflection and discussion from each lesson to talk over as a group.

5. Ask the group members to name one thing they have most appreciated about the way the group has worked during this Bible study. Ask group members to discuss any changes they might suggest in the way the group works in future studies.

6. Invite group members to complete lessons 25 through 30 on their own during the six days before the next meeting. They should write out their own answers to the questions as preparation for next week's session.

7. Discuss with group members ways in which studying Handel's *Messiah* manifests the power of music to proclaim the gospel of salvation.

8. Conclude by praying aloud together the prayer at the end of one of the lessons discussed. You may want to conclude the prayer by asking members to voice prayers of thanksgiving.

"O that my words were written down! O that they were inscribed in a book! O that with an iron pen and with lead they were engraved on a rock forever!" JOB 19:23–24

Confident Trust in the Redeemer

45. ARIA (Soprano)

I know that my Redeemer liveth, and that He shall stand at the latter day upon the earth; and though worms destroy this body, yet in my flesh shall I see God. For now is Christ risen from the dead, the firstfruits of them that sleep. (Job 19:25, 26; 1 Corinthians 15:20)

JOB 19:19–29

19 *All my intimate friends abhor me,*
and those whom I loved have turned against me.
20 *My bones cling to my skin and to my flesh,*
and I have escaped by the skin of my teeth.
21 *Have pity on me, have pity on me, O you my friends,*
for the hand of God has touched me!
22 *Why do you, like God, pursue me,*
never satisfied with my flesh?

23 *"O that my words were written down!*
O that they were inscribed in a book!
24 *O that with an iron pen and with lead*

they were engraved on a rock forever!
25*For I know that my Redeemer lives,*
and that at the last he will stand upon the earth;
26*and after my skin has been thus destroyed,*
then in my flesh I shall see God,
27*whom I shall see on my side,*
and my eyes shall behold, and not another.
My heart faints within me!
28*If you say, 'How we will persecute him!'*
and, 'The root of the matter is found in him';
29*be afraid of the sword,*
for wrath brings the punishment of the sword,
so that you may know there is a judgment."

Many who are unfamiliar with *Messiah* assume that the flourish of the Hallelujah chorus is the conclusion of Handel's oratorio. He certainly could have quit there; the chorus would serve as a powerful finale. But Part 3 continues the work with a meditation on the consequences of Christ's saving work for humanity and the world. The final nine movements focus on the bodily resurrection of all believers and the eternal life we will share with God forever.

The soprano aria expresses the certain belief that because Christ lives, we shall live. The melody and tempo, accompanied by unison violins, are serene and majestic. The words "I know" express a splendid confidence that is wonderfully reassuring. The aria displays the full range of the soprano's voice and presents a ringing declaration of hope in the future resurrection of the dead. This Messiah, who is the King of glory and the Lord or lords, is also "my Redeemer," the one who gives the hope of eternal life to every individual believer.

At the time the book of Job was written, the faith of Israel had not yet developed a belief in resurrection or eternal life. The character of Job had lost his home, his family, and finally his health in one disaster after another. His so-called friends insist that he must have sinned to deserve such a fate. In this passage, Job exclaims that he is reduced to skin and bones and has barely escaped death (verse 20). He turns to his friends in his anguish and pleads for their sympathy (verse 21). In his desperate feelings of abandonment, he clings to his last and final hope. In a message that he wants written in stone to last forever (verses 23–24), Job proclaims his firm confidence that someday, somehow, he will be vindicated by God.

A "redeemer" (*go'el*, in Hebrew) in Israelite society was a person, generally the next-of-kin, who came to avenge a great injustice against another or to vindicate that person from blame and punishment. The word is used frequently in the Old Testament for God as the redeemer of his people: for example, "O Lord, my rock and my redeemer" (Ps 19:14) and "Our Redeemer—the Lord of hosts is his name—is the Holy One of Israel" (Isa 47:4). Job imagines that after his death, God will make known his blamelessness and vindicate his assertions of innocence. Scholars debate whether Job is referring here to some type of bodily life after death. But surely Job is expressing a hopeful affirmation of God's ultimate justice and confidence in a restored relationship in which God is not estranged from him. In a visionary moment, Job saw God on his side, defending him amid his undeserved suffering.

Messiah has chosen texts from the Old Testament that present God as a king, a warrior, a shepherd, and here a redeemer, then applied these metaphors to Christ. The Christian knows what Job could not know—that Christ has passed from death to resurrected life, and that God will raise our mortal bodies to life as well. Christ fulfills the ancient Israelite role of the redeemer-vindicator in the fullest possible way. To make clear the fulfillment of the ancient passage from Job, the aria adds this verse from Paul's writings: "For now is Christ risen from the dead." Truly he is the just Redeemer and Vindicator of everyone who experiences life as distressed, anguished, desperate, and discouraging.

Reflection and discussion

- How do the words and music instill confidence in me for future resurrection and eternal life?

- What do I think about the assumption of Job's "friends" that Job's suffering must be caused by some prior sin? Have I ever assumed this about another person?

- Why does Job think his situation is unjust? Have I ever thought about my life in this way?

- Do I believe that my future life will involve the resurrection of my body? What are the implications of this belief for me?

Prayer

Redeemer and Lord, I know that you have risen from the dead as the assurance that I will follow. Give me hope in the midst of life's distressing trials. Help me to believe that you are a God of justice and that you are faithful to all your promises.

For he must reign until he has put all his enemies under his feet. The last enemy to be destroyed is death. For "God has put all things in subjection under his feet." 1 CORINTHIANS 15:25–27

Forgiveness and Life in Christ

46. CHORUS

Since by man came death, by man also the resurrection of the dead. For as in Adam all die, even so in Christ shall all be made alive. (1 Corinthians 15:21, 22)

1 CORINTHIANS 15:17–28 [17]*If Christ has not been raised, your faith is futile*
and you are still in your sins. [18]*Then those also who have died in Christ have per-*
ished. [19]*If for this life only we have hoped in Christ, we are of all people most to*
be pitied.

[20]*But in fact Christ has been raised from the dead, the first fruits of those who*
have died. [21]*For since death came through a human being, the resurrection of the*
dead has also come through a human being; [22]*for as all die in Adam, so all will be*
made alive in Christ. [23]*But each in his own order: Christ the first fruits, then at his*
coming those who belong to Christ. [24]*Then comes the end, when he hands over the*
kingdom to God the Father, after he has destroyed every ruler and every authority
and power. [25]*For he must reign until he has put all his enemies under his feet.* [26]*The*
last enemy to be destroyed is death. [27]*For "God has put all things in subjection*
under his feet." But when it says, "All things are put in subjection," it is plain that
this does not include the one who put all things in subjection under him. [28]*When*

all things are subjected to him, then the Son himself will also be subjected to the one who put all things in subjection under him, so that God may be all in all.

The chorus applies the confident affirmation of the soprano aria to all humanity. Because our Redeemer lives, we too will be raised from death. The contrasts within the chorus couldn't be stronger: between death and risen life, pianissimo and fortissimo, adagio and allegro. The primordial sentence of death is chanted without accompaniment in muted, ponderous tones, while the resurrection of humanity is sung with stunning energy. So great was the Messiah's victory that he has reversed the inevitability of our eternal death.

In this chapter of the first letter to the Corinthians, Paul offers the most thorough discussion in the Bible of the resurrection of the dead. The new glorious existence foretold by the prophets and sages of Israel, which was expected to occur in the final age, has suddenly, unexpectedly begun in Christ. This belief in resurrection is the bedrock of Christian faith (verse 17). Without it, Christianity is only a system of delusions and futile human fantasy, leaving its adherents "most to be pitied" (verse 19). So, sweeping away all the gloomy consequences that follow from denying the resurrection, Paul triumphantly declares: "But in fact Christ has been raised from the dead" (verse 20).

Paul describes Christ's resurrection as "the first fruits of those who have died" (verses 20, 23). The "first fruits" is a term from the sacrificial system of Israel. The first produce of the fields and orchards were dedicated to God, ensuring the blessings of God on the remainder of the harvest to come. The firstborn child was also dedicated to God, and Israel is often described in the Hebrew Scriptures as God's "firstborn." By calling Christ the "first fruits of them that sleep," Paul professes that Christ's resurrection is the anticipatory guarantee of the harvest to come, the future resurrection of all.

In contrasting Adam and Christ, Paul takes up the teaching of the Jewish rabbis that all humanity is involved in the sin and punishment of Adam. But he deduces that deliverance from death has come about by the involvement of Christ in all humanity (verses 21–22). Just as Adam is a representational figure of failed humanity, the risen Christ represents renewed humanity.

Through human solidarity with Adam, death came into the world; through solidarity with Christ will come the resurrection of the dead.

Paul portrays salvation as a great drama in which Christ gains victory over all the forces arrayed in opposition to God. The "last enemy" to be subdued by Christ is death itself (verses 24–26). In the resurrection of Christ, death's fate is sealed, but death is still active in creation until its final defeat. Then, at the end, all who belong to Christ will be raised to life again, and Christ will hand over the kingdom to the Father so that God alone will be sovereign over all creation (verses 24, 28).

We live now in the interval between Christ's resurrection and the day of Christ's coming when the dead will be raised to life. The time of forgiveness, restoration, and victory over sin and death has already come upon the earth through the resurrection of Christ. The future age has already burst into the present age, so that we live now with a mixture of fulfillment and expectation. What happened when Christ rose from the tomb has made the world a different place and has given us the possibility to become a different kind of people.

Reflection and discussion

- In what ways do I experience solidarity with the rest of humanity? In what way is that solidarity transformed through my incorporation into the body of Christ?

- What is most convincing in Paul's argument that belief in resurrection is the bedrock of Christian faith?

- How does the image of the "first fruits" indicate the relationship of Christ's resurrection to our own?

- In what ways does Handel contrast the death that comes in Adam and the resurrection that comes in Christ?

- In what way is the present age a time of both fulfillment and expectation? What is the difference between wishful thinking and Christian hope?

Prayer

Risen Christ, you are risen from the dead and you are my hope of resurrection. Without you I am trapped in sin and destined for eternal death. Because of you, death's fate is sealed and I can live in joyful hope.

As was the man of dust, so are those who are of the dust; and as is the man of heaven, so are those who are of heaven. Just as we have borne the image of the man of dust, we will also bear the image of the man of heaven. 1 CORINTHIANS 15:48–49

Transformed in the Gloriously Risen Lord

47. RECITATIVE (Bass)

Behold, I tell you a mystery. We shall not all sleep, but we shall all be changed in a moment, in the twinkling of an eye, at the last trumpet. (1 Corinthians 15:51, 52)

48. ARIA (Bass)

The trumpet shall sound, and the dead shall be raised incorruptible, and we shall be changed. For this corruptible must put on incorruption, and this mortal must put on immortality. (1 Corinthians 15:52, 53)

1 CORINTHIANS 15:42–53 [42]*So it is with the resurrection of the dead. What*
is sown is perishable, what is raised is imperishable. [43]*It is sown in dishonor, it is*
raised in glory. It is sown in weakness, it is raised in power. [44]*It is sown a physical*
body, it is raised a spiritual body. If there is a physical body, there is also a spiri-
tual body. [45]*Thus it is written, "The first man, Adam, became a living being"; the*
last Adam became a life-giving spirit. [46]*But it is not the spiritual that is first, but*
the physical, and then the spiritual. [47]*The first man was from the earth, a man of*
dust; the second man is from heaven. [48]*As was the man of dust, so are those who*

are of the dust; and as is the man of heaven, so are those who are of heaven. [49]*Just as we have borne the image of the man of dust, we will also bear the image of the man of heaven.*

[50]*What I am saying, brothers and sisters, is this: flesh and blood cannot inherit the kingdom of God, nor does the perishable inherit the imperishable.* [51]*Listen, I will tell you a mystery! We will not all die, but we will all be changed,* [52]*in a moment, in the twinkling of an eye, at the last trumpet. For the trumpet will sound, and the dead will be raised imperishable, and we will be changed.* [53]*For this perishable body must put on imperishability, and this mortal body must put on immortality.*

The bass recitative forms a transition between the last chorus, proclaiming the certainty of resurrection in Christ, and the bass aria, anticipating the dramatic events associated with the resurrection of the dead at the end of time. The bass begins quietly, revealing the "mystery" hidden in God until the coming of Christ: "We shall all be changed in a moment." Then suddenly we hear the trumpet sound, the only instrumental solo in the work. The bass aria summons the dead to life and announces the transformation of our bodies. The dialogue between the bass voice and the trumpet is forceful and convincing as it anticipates the day when Christ will come in glory.

Many to whom Paul wrote naively assumed that the resurrection of the dead means the resuscitation of corrupted corpses. Paul explains that resurrection involves a complete transformation of the body into a new and glorious state. Like a plant that springs forth from a seed or a butterfly that emerges from a cocoon, our bodies will be radically changed to make them suitable for a new form of existence. The body in this present life is perishable and weak; the body of those resurrected from the dead will be imperishable and glorious (verses 42–44). Paul again uses the representational figures of Adam and Christ to contrast humanity in its natural life and in its spiritual life to come. We inherit one kind of body and life from Adam, "the man of dust," followed by a renewed, transformed body from Christ, "the man of heaven" (verses 45–49). We await the day when Christ, manifested in his resurrected body, will come from heaven to raise us and transform us into his likeness.

In the ancient world, the sounding of the trumpet was a signal that the king was about to emerge from his chamber and enter the throne room to take his seat on the throne. As the trumpet sounded, all stood in his honor. Here the trumpet signals the end of all things as we have known it. It spreads its awesome sound through the regions of the dead, calling everyone to come before the throne of Christ. The Messiah is taking his place as the Lord of God's kingdom, and all are raised to life.

Belief in "the resurrection of the body and the life of the world to come" is a central teaching of Paul and the final doctrine expressed in the church's ancient creeds. The "how" of resurrection still remains a "mystery" that human words and images cannot express. Yet, we know that God's plan for the end is not to destroy our bodies and start again but to transform our bodies, not to reject his creation but to redeem it. We know that on the day of Christ's glory we will all be changed, and our perishable, mortal bodies will put on imperishability and immortality (verse 53). Metaphors and analogies can take us only so far. No human logic can contain the mysteries of faith. We must finally just give up the attempts of reason and sing with joy at what we have been promised. This is what Handel's *Messiah* leads us to do in its remaining movements as it proclaims our eternal share in the victory of Christ.

Reflection and discussion

- What is the connection between the resurrection of Christ and my own victory over death?

- What is the purpose of the long melismas that fall on the word "changed"?

- What is the difference between resuscitation and resurrection? Why is faith necessary to accept the reality of resurrection from the dead?

- What is the effect of the trumpet on my understanding and appreciation of the bass aria?

- How do the words "incorruption" and "immortality" offer me hope? How do they express a reality that images cannot communicate?

Prayer

Victorious Lord, when the trumpet sounds for your glorious coming, we will be raised incorruptible. Thank you for the promise of eternal life and the hope for the future that you have instilled within me.

Therefore, my beloved, be steadfast, immovable, always excelling in the work of the Lord, because you know that in the Lord your labor is not in vain. 1 CORINTHIANS 15:58

Death Is Swallowed Up in Victory

49. RECITATIVE (Alto)

Then shall be brought to pass the saying that is written: Death is swallowed up in victory! (1 Corinthians 15:54)

50. DUET (Alto and Tenor)

O death, where is thy sting? O grave, where is thy victory? The sting of death is sin, and the strength of sin is the law. (1 Corinthians 15:55, 56)

51. CHORUS

But thanks be to God, who giveth us the victory through our Lord Jesus Christ. (1 Corinthians 15:57)

1 CORINTHIANS 15:54–58 [54]*When this perishable body puts on imperishability, and this mortal body puts on immortality, then the saying that is written will be fulfilled:*

> *"Death has been swallowed up in victory."*
> [55]*"Where, O death, is your victory?*
> *Where, O death, is your sting?"*

[56]*The sting of death is sin, and the power of sin is the law.* [57]*But thanks be to God, who gives us the victory through our Lord Jesus Christ.*

[58]*Therefore, my beloved, be steadfast, immovable, always excelling in the work of the Lord, because you know that in the Lord your labor is not in vain.*

Paul's teaching on the resurrection of humanity ends with a great cry of "victory." Paul uses the word "victory" only three times in all his letters, and all three occurrences are in these few lines (verses 54, 55, 57). The triumph of the Messiah has neutralized the forces of death and the grave. All that is left in the story of redemption is to proclaim the news and encourage the world to share in its benefits.

The alto recitative refers to a saying that is written in the prophets: "Death is swallowed up in victory!" This quote derives from Isaiah in a passage celebrating God's future deliverance for his people and his triumph over death:

> [6]*On this mountain the Lord of hosts will make for all peoples*
> *a feast of rich food, a feast of well-aged wines,*
> *of rich food filled with marrow, of well-aged wines strained clear.*
> [7]*And he will destroy on this mountain*
> *the shroud that is cast over all peoples,*
> *the sheet that is spread over all nations;*
> *he will swallow up death forever.*
> [8]*Then the Lord God will wipe away the tears from all faces,*
> *and the disgrace of his people he will take away from all the earth,*
> *for the Lord has spoken.*
> [9]*It will be said on that day,*
> *Lo, this is our God; we have waited for him, so that he might save us.*
> *This is the Lord for whom we have waited;*
> *let us be glad and rejoice in his salvation.*
> [10]*For the hand of the Lord will rest on this mountain.* ***Isaiah 25:6–10***

An old metaphor depicts death as a gaping cavern that swallowed up all living things (see Prov 1:12; Isa 5:14). Here the image is reversed: death itself is swallowed up (Isa 25:8). "Forever," says Isaiah; "in victory," writes Paul. The "shroud" that covers the people is death. Perhaps God will use that very shroud to wipe away the tears from the faces of all people (Isa 25:8). Isaiah presents a wonderful image of God's victory over death, the salvation for which God's people have waited (Isa 25:9). It is this day of salvation in which death is conquered that Paul proclaims to be fulfilled in Christ.

Paul's famous taunt of death, "Where, O death, is your victory? Where, O death, is your sting?" is sung in *Messiah*'s only duet. Alto and tenor alternately sing the verses, delicately ridiculing death in an imitative style. "Death" and "grave" are personified and addressed by the taunting tune. The reign of death and the supremacy of the grave (*sheol,* in Hebrew) are indeed ended. The victory belongs to God's Messiah.

Paul's words refer to another ancient prophet. In the words of Hosea, God is wrathfully calling upon the powers of Death and Sheol to punish sinful Israel:

Shall I ransom them from the power of Sheol?
  Shall I redeem them from Death?
O Death, where are your plagues?
  O Sheol, where is your destruction?
  Compassion is hidden from my eyes. **Hosea 13:14**

Here, in the ancient prophet, the questions are rhetorical: God indeed will not ransom his people from the power of Sheol; he will not redeem them from Death. Rather, God summons Death and Sheol to come and carry out their work of destruction.

Paul's use of this passage is extraordinary because he makes the prophet's words say the exact opposite of what Hosea intended. The call for Death and Sheol to destroy is transformed into a triumphal taunt over the defeat of death and the grave. Death's stinging power to evoke fear and despair is definitively defeated in the resurrection of the dead. The trumpet summons the living and the dead, announcing the Messiah's decisive victory.

The chorus sings Paul's joyful thanksgiving: "But thanks be to God, who giveth us the victory through our Lord Jesus Christ" (verse 57). The present tense is significant: the fruit of God's victory through Christ is still being worked out in the world. Each day we share in that victory, drawing on its power for our daily struggles against failure, doubt, and guilt. God gives us the victory each day; we don't have to earn it, pay for it, or fight for it. Thanks be to God, the victory that has been won on our behalf is ours to claim each day. Therefore, we can do the work of the Lord with confidence, knowing that in him everything we do has ultimate meaning and purpose (verse 58). Nothing we do in Christ is ever "in vain."

Reflection and discussion

- Which words of Paul are most comforting for me? In what way do they take away the sting of death?

- How does Paul's teaching about resurrection lead me to do what he urges in verse 58?

- Handel's tombstone contains these words of Job: "I know that my Redeemer liveth." What words of *Messiah* would I choose for my own epitaph?

Prayer

Thanks be to God who gives us the victory through our Lord Jesus Christ. You have destroyed the powers of death and given us hope and confidence for the future. Help me live a life that is worth living for eternity.

LESSON 29 SESSION 6

Who will separate us from the love of Christ? Will hardship, or distress, or persecution, or famine, or nakedness, or peril, or sword? No, in all these things we are more than conquerors through him who loved us.

ROMANS 8:35, 37

Confidence in God's Eternal Love

52. ARIA (Soprano or Alto)

If God be for us, who can be against us? Who shall lay anything to the charge of God's elect? It is God that justifieth. Who is he that condemneth? It is Christ that died, yea rather, that is risen again, who is at the right hand of God, who makes intercession for us. (Romans 8:31, 33, 34)

ROMANS 8:31–39 [31]*What then are we to say about these things? If God is for*
us, who is against us? [32]*He who did not withhold his own Son, but gave him up for*
all of us, will he not with him also give us everything else? [33]*Who will bring any*
charge against God's elect? It is God who justifies. [34]*Who is to condemn? It is Christ*
Jesus, who died, yes, who was raised, who is at the right hand of God, who indeed
intercedes for us. [35]*Who will separate us from the love of Christ? Will hardship, or*
distress, or persecution, or famine, or nakedness, or peril, or sword? [36]*As it is written,*

> *"For your sake we are being killed all day long;*
> *we are accounted as sheep to be slaughtered."*

[37]*No, in all these things we are more than conquerors through him who loved us.*
[38]*For I am convinced that neither death, nor life, nor angels, nor rulers, nor things*
present, nor things to come, nor powers, [39]*nor height, nor depth, nor anything else in*
all creation, will be able to separate us from the love of God in Christ Jesus our Lord.

Handel's final aria is sung by the soprano: "If God be for us, who can be against us?" The librettist has chosen verses from Paul's most eloquent expression of Christian confidence and comfort, the eighth chapter of his letter to the Romans on the surety of God's grace. The words and phrases of the aria are colored with dramatic emphasis to accentuate its confident tone.

The first question sets the theme for the following verses: If God is on our side, who or what could possibly mount any effective threat against us (verse 31)? The indisputable evidence that God is on our side is of course that he gave up his own Son for us. And if God was willing to bestow such a priceless gift upon us, could there be anything he would withhold from us (verse 32)? The remainder of the passage emphatically demonstrates that the answer to this question is an unqualified No! "God is for us"—this disarmingly simple truth is the gospel in a nutshell.

The next question continues along the same lines: Who would bring a charge against us and who could possibly condemn us (verses 33–34)? Paul shows that the only ones who have the power to accuse or condemn us are God, who has in fact acquitted us, or Christ, who has already conquered death, the ultimate condemnation. If our only potential accusers are our strongest benefactors, then truly we have nothing to ultimately fear.

God is indeed "for us," and he has verified his stance toward us in the person of Jesus Christ who died, was raised to life, and is now at the right hand of God, interceding for us (verse 34). This chain of statements demonstrating the Messiah's saving love for us concludes this final solo of Handel's oratorio. The one who "died" has redeemed humanity from sin and all its consequences. The one who "is risen again" assures us of victory over death and gives us the pledge of eternal life. The one who "is at the right hand of God" attests that Christ is enthroned with power and reigns over all creation. The one who "makes intercession for us" employs his divine power before God on our behalf.

Paul's final question is not sung in the aria but brings his confident assertions to a close: "Who will separate us from the love of Christ?" (verse 35). Paul lists several physical adversities, many of which recall the sufferings of Job and even of Paul himself. Though Christ has conquered all the powers that oppress us, still the struggle on earth continues. The church endures suffering, persecution, and even martyrdom, yet "in all these things we are more than conquerors through him who loved us" (verse 37). Our distress and tribulations serve God's saving purposes when we offer them to God in union with the sacrifice of Christ. God works through our suffering to give us the victory.

Paul's astonishing confidence assures us that nothing natural or supernatural in all of creation can frustrate God's merciful love for us (verses 38–39). His list of physical threats is heightened to cosmic powers: death or life, good or evil angels, the present or the future, height or depth—all dimensions of reality, even time and space. "I am convinced," Paul states with unshakable conviction, that absolutely nothing "will be able to separate us from the love of God in Christ Jesus our Lord." Armed with such secure faith in God's love, we can face the future with confident hope.

Reflection and discussion

- What are the practical implications for me of Paul's confident proclamation that "God is for us"?

- Which of the threats of verses 35 and 38 are most real to me? Why can they not separate me from God's love?

- Why is this final aria of *Messiah* a text that I need to hear often and listen to well?

Prayer

Lord Jesus Christ, you reign over all the threatening powers of creation. Through your death and resurrection you have demonstrated the trustworthiness and fidelity of God's love. In the face of life's trials and tragedies, assure me that nothing can separate me from that love.

Then I heard every creature in heaven and on earth and under the earth and in the sea, and all that is in them, singing, "To the one seated on the throne and to the Lamb be blessing and honor and glory and might forever and ever!" REVELATION 5:13

Worthy Is the Lamb that Was Slain

53. CHORUS

Worthy is the Lamb that was slain, and hath redeemed us to God by His blood, to receive power, and riches, and wisdom, and strength, and honour, and glory, and blessing. Blessing and honour, glory and power, be unto Him that sitteth upon the throne, and unto the Lamb, for ever and ever. Amen. (Revelation 5:12, 9, 13)

REVELATION 5:1–14 [1]*Then I saw in the right hand of the one seated on the*
throne a scroll written on the inside and on the back, sealed with seven seals; [2]*and*
I saw a mighty angel proclaiming with a loud voice, "Who is worthy to open the
scroll and break its seals?" [3]*And no one in heaven or on earth or under the earth*
was able to open the scroll or to look into it. [4]*And I began to weep bitterly because*
no one was found worthy to open the scroll or to look into it. [5]*Then one of the elders*
said to me, "Do not weep. See, the Lion of the tribe of Judah, the Root of David, has
conquered, so that he can open the scroll and its seven seals."

[6]*Then I saw between the throne and the four living creatures and among the*
elders a Lamb standing as if it had been slaughtered, having seven horns and seven
eyes, which are the seven spirits of God sent out into all the earth. [7]*He went and*

took the scroll from the right hand of the one who was seated on the throne. [8]When he had taken the scroll, the four living creatures and the twenty-four elders fell before the Lamb, each holding a harp and golden bowls full of incense, which are the prayers of the saints. [9]They sing a new song:

"You are worthy to take the scroll
and to open its seals,
for you were slaughtered and by your blood you ransomed for God
saints from every tribe and language and people and nation;
[10]you have made them to be a kingdom and priests serving our God,
and they will reign on earth."

[11]Then I looked, and I heard the voice of many angels surrounding the throne and the living creatures and the elders; they numbered myriads of myriads and thousands of thousands, [12]singing with full voice,

"Worthy is the Lamb that was slaughtered
to receive power and wealth and wisdom and might
and honor and glory and blessing!"

[13]Then I heard every creature in heaven and on earth and under the earth and in the sea, and all that is in them, singing,

"To the one seated on the throne and to the Lamb
be blessing and honor and glory and might
forever and ever!"

[14]And the four living creatures said, "Amen!" And the elders fell down and worshiped.

The last choral piece of *Messiah*, "Worthy is the Lamb," like the Hallelujah chorus, is taken from the Bible's last book, Revelation. Trumpet and timpani return to punctuate this expansive finale. The adagio tempo at the opening allows all the voices and instruments to sound to the fullest. It is appropriate that this final movement be sung by the full chorus since Revelation suggests that all the creatures of heaven and earth worship the enthroned Lamb. The chorus sings, but we are drawn along with all creation into this praise of the Messiah who has redeemed us.

The scroll with the seven seals in God's right hand symbolizes the divine plan to redeem the world (verse 1). A search throughout all creation finds no one worthy to break the seals and open the scroll—that is, to carry out God's plan for the world's salvation (verses 2–3). Then an elder declares that "the Lion of the tribe of Judah, the Root of David" could open the scroll because he has "conquered" (verse 5). This Hebrew symbol of the Messiah, expressing his lion-like strength and ferocious power, is ironically transformed into the image of the Lamb. Rather than the lion who tears his prey, Jesus the Messiah is the Lamb who is torn by the powers who oppose his reign. Symbolized by the Lamb who is slaughtered yet now standing (verse 6), the risen Messiah bears the marks of his suffering and shows that sacrificial love is the way to conquer the foes of God's saving plan. The Lamb's seven horns and seven eyes, in apocalyptic symbolism, express Christ's perfect power and perfect wisdom. The Lamb takes the scroll and opens it, demonstrating that Christ accomplished the divine plan written upon it.

Like the blood of the Passover lamb which protected the Israelites from the plague of death, the blood of the Lamb of God ransomed people of every language and nation (verse 9). The church on earth worships with the assembly of heaven in divine liturgy focused on the Lamb. The whole universe expresses a seven-fold praise of God and the Lamb: power, wealth, wisdom, might, honor, glory, and blessing (verse 12).

The great "Amen" (verse 14) is lavishly sung, first by the basses, then the tenors, altos, and the whole chorus in a hymn of triumphant praise. Far more than simply a traditional way to end worship, the final Amen is an invitation to all of us to affirm the message of *Messiah*. Amen is a Hebrew word that has been kept in its original language by the Greek authors of the New Testament and by every language of Christian worship. It implies truth and steadfastness, and in Christian liturgy it expresses solemn ratification of expressions of faith. The climactic Amen commits us to the truth that has been sung and celebrated through the Scriptures in Handel's work. As we conclude our study of *Messiah*, let us give praise to God, as Handel himself inscribed at the conclusion of his musical score: *Solo Deo Gloria*, "To God alone the glory."

Reflection and discussion

- What does it matter that the angels and saints of heaven praise God with me? What are the implications of this cosmic liturgy for my Sunday worship?

- Why is the Messiah depicted as a Lamb rather than a Lion? What does this tell me about the way he conquers?

- Why is the Lamb alone worthy to take the scroll and open its seals? In what way does Handel's *Messiah* sing of the contents of that heavenly scroll?

Prayer

Glorious Lamb who reigns in glory, you were slain and redeemed us with your blood. You are worthy to receive power and wealth, wisdom and might, honor, glory and blessing. Penetrate my heart through the inspired texts of this oratorio and lead me to worship you forever with all the choirs of heaven.

SUGGESTIONS FOR FACILITATORS, GROUP SESSION 6

1. Welcome group members and make any final announcements or requests.

2. You may want to pray this prayer as a group:
Lord and Redeemer, without you we are trapped in sin and destined for eternal death. Yet, you are victorious over all the threatening forces of the universe, proving the trustworthiness of your promises and the fidelity of divine love. In the face of life's trials and tragedies, assure us that nothing can separate us from that love, and give us confidence in an unending future with you. Penetrate our hearts through the inspired texts of Scripture and the music of Handel's oratorio and lead us to worship you forever with all the choirs of heaven.

3. Ask one or both of the following questions:
    - How has this study of Handel's *Messiah* deepened your life in Christ?
    - In what way has this study challenged you the most?

4. Discuss lessons 25 through 30. Choose one or more of the questions for reflection and discussion from each lesson to discuss as a group.

5. Ask the group if they would like to study another title in the Threshold Bible Study series. Discuss the topic and dates, and make a decision among those interested. Ask the group members to suggest people they would like to invite to participate in the next study series.

6. Ask the group to discuss the insights that stand out most from this study over the past six weeks.

7. Conclude by praying aloud the following prayer or another of your own choosing:
Holy Spirit of the living God, you inspired the writers of the Scriptures, and you have guided our study during these weeks. Continue to deepen our love for the word of God in the holy Scriptures and draw us more deeply into the heart of Jesus. Thank you for your merciful, gracious, steadfast, and faithful love.

Ordering Additional Studies

AVAILABLE TITLES IN THIS SERIES INCLUDE...

- Advent Light
- Angels of God
- Divine Mercy
- Eucharist
- The Feasts of Judaism
- Forgiveness
- God's Spousal Love
- The Holy Spirit and Spiritual Gifts
- Jerusalem, the Holy City
- Mary, Royal Mother of the Messiah
- The Mass
- Missionary Discipleship
- Music, Hymns, and Canticles
- Mysteries of the Rosary
- The Names of Jesus
- Parables of Jesus
- Peacemaking and Nonviolence
- People of the Passion
- Pilgrimage in the Footsteps of Jesus
- Psalms of the Evening
- Psalms of the Morning
- Questions Jesus Asks
- The Resurrection and the Life
- The Sacred Heart of Jesus
- Stewardship of the Earth
- The Tragic and Triumphant Cross
- Wholehearted Commitment
  PART 1: Deuteronomy 1–15
  PART 2: Deuteronomy 16–34
- Jesus, the Messianic King
  PART 1: Matthew 1–16
  PART 2: Matthew 17–28
- Jesus, the Suffering Servant
  PART 1: Mark 1–8
  PART 2: Mark 9–16
- Jesus, the Compassionate Savior
  PART 1: Luke 1–11
  PART 2: Luke 12–24
- Jesus, the Word Made Flesh
  PART 1: John 1–10
  PART 2: John 11–21
- Church of the Holy Spirit
  PART 1: Acts of the Apostles 1–14
  PART 2: Acts of the Apostles 15–28
- Salvation Offered for All People: Romans
- Proclaiming Christ Crucified: 1 Corinthians
- Unity in Christ's Church: Colossians, Philemon, Ephesians
- New Covenant Worship: Hebrews
- Faith, Hope, and Love: The Seven Catholic Epistles
- The Lamb and the Beasts: The Book of Revelation

TO CHECK AVAILABILITY OR FOR A DESCRIPTION OF EACH STUDY, VISIT OUR WEBSITE AT **www.ThresholdBibleStudy.com** OR CALL US AT **1-800-321-0411**